THE PRICE
OF *Nice*

Why Comfort Keeps Us Stuck
—and 4 Actions for Real Change

AMIRA BARGER

Berrett–Koehler Publishers, Inc.

Berrett-Koehler Publishers, Inc.
1333 Broadway, Suite P100
Oakland, CA 94612-1921
Tel: (510) 817-2277
Fax: (510) 817-2278
bkconnection.com

ORDERING INFORMATION

Quantity sales. Special discounts are available on quantity purchases by corporations, associations, and others. For details, please go to bkconnection.com to see our bulk discounts or contact bookorders@bkpub.com for more information.

Individual sales. Berrett-Koehler publications are available through most bookstores. They can also be ordered directly from Berrett-Koehler: Tel: (800) 929-2929; Fax: (802) 864-7626; bkconnection.com.

Orders for college textbook / course adoption use. Please contact Berrett-Koehler: Tel: (800) 929-2929; Fax: (802) 864-7626.

Distributed to the US trade and internationally by Penguin Random House Publisher Services.

The authorized representative in the EU for product safety and compliance is EU Compliance Partner, Pärnu mnt. 139b-14, 11317 Tallinn, Estonia, www.eucompliancepartner.com, +372 5368 65 02.

Berrett-Koehler and the BK logo are registered trademarks of Berrett-Koehler Publishers, Inc.

Printed in the United States of America

Berrett-Koehler books are printed on long-lasting acid-free paper. When it is available, we choose paper that has been manufactured by environmentally responsible processes. These may include using trees grown in sustainable forests, incorporating recycled paper, minimizing chlorine in bleaching, or recycling the energy produced at the paper mill.

Library of Congress Cataloging-in-Publication Data

Names: Barger, Amira author
Title: The price of nice : why comfort keeps us stuck-and 4 actions for real change / Amira Barger.
Description: First edition. | Oakland, CA : Berrett-Koehler Publishers, Inc, [2025] | Includes bibliographical references and index.
Identifiers: LCCN 2025018400 (print) | LCCN 2025018401 (ebook) | ISBN 9798890571137 paperback | ISBN 9798890571144 pdf | ISBN 9798890571151 epub
Subjects: LCSH: Organizational change | Business communication | Psychology, Industrial
Classification: LCC HD58.8 .B368 2025 (print) | LCC HD58.8 (ebook) | DDC 658.4/06—dc23/eng/20250717
LC record available at https://lccn.loc.gov/2025018400
LC ebook record available at https://lccn.loc.gov/2025018401

First Edition
33 32 31 30 29 28 27 26 25   10 9 8 7 6 5 4 3 2 1

Book production: Happenstance Type-O-Rama
Cover design: Ashley Ingram
Author photos by Eugeniya Pasterskaya, Door into Summer Photography
Amira is wearing Argent

To nine-year-old Amira—don't worry, babe. You find your nerve again.

●

To my daughter, Audrey—in you, I see the bold, unapologetic, and transformative force I once feared and now admire, the kind of person the world so desperately needs.

●

To my partner in life, Jonathan—your unwavering support and steadfast growth alongside me have been an anchor. Thank you for holding space for my voice, for my dreams, and for every step of this journey.

●

To everyone striving to embrace who they are—uninterrupted—this book is for you.

CONTENTS

Part IV: REVISIT

PREFACE

I'm an '80s baby, but the '90s raised me. I grew up with parents who maintained discipline through sharp looks, heavy sighs, a raised eyebrow that could stop you mid-sentence, and the occasional swift rebuke to the backside. Nice wasn't a suggestion; it was a nonnegotiable demand.

And, for much of my life, I lived up to it. I was known to many as "Precious, Sweet Amira." In fact, my husband's late mother, Pearl, used to enthusiastically address me by that title as if it were my full name. I leaned into the persona, wearing it like a badge of honor. But that existence came with a price.

The problem was, *nice* never quite fit me. It was an unrelenting tug-of-war between the suffocating expectations of the daughter I was supposed to be and the daughter I truly was—the one who asked questions, wanting to be heard, not just seen. For a long time, it was a trap I couldn't figure out how to free myself from.

Growing up, doing things "for the 'gram" didn't exist yet. The one surefire way to showcase that you'd just lived your best life on a summer adventure somewhere? *Vacation hair.* If you know, you know. It screamed, *"I went somewhere fabulous, and I need you to know it!"*

My sisters and I had two best friends, blonde-haired, hazel-eyed twins who were fixtures at our house, and we at theirs.

The twins would return from vacation every summer, grinning ear to ear, with braided cornrows, beads clacking together, and painfully sunburned scalps. But soon, their cornrows were more like frizzy haystacks, and they'd be sitting cross-legged on my mom's bedroom floor, begging her to rebraid them.

"Can you braid it like theirs?" they would ask, pointing at my sisters and me.

My mom would sigh, shake her head slightly, and get to work. As she'd done a thousand times before, she'd pull out her comb, part the twins' fine blonde hair into sections, and start braiding while they squirmed, winced, and squealed.

"Ouch! That's too tight!"

"Why does it hurt so much?"

"Does it hurt like this when you get yours done, too?"

"Is my hair falling out? I think my hair is falling out!"

Standing in the doorway, brow furrowed, I watched these girls act like they were being tortured. You know those scenes in cartoons where the character is trying to make a decision, with an angel on one shoulder and a demon on the other, both giving advice? I'd spent most of my life trying to choke out that little demon voice. But that day, I was done with the drama. It was too much, and the dark side took over. It felt like an out-of-body experience. As if channeling the wisdom from an ancestral Black auntie, I matter-of-factly blurted out, "It's because *your* hair isn't made for braids!"

The room fell silent amidst a collective gasp. My mom froze, hands mid-braid, with an unmistakable look that conveyed all it needed to. I could almost hear her gritted teeth through her *"Amira, I know you didn't just say that"* stare. My youngest sister stifled a giggle while the rest looked on with pity, imagining the whooping I'd get later.

One of the twins whipped her head around so fast that beads went flying everywhere, her eyes wide, her mouth open, her expression a mixture of shock, hurt, and confusion. But I wasn't done. I crossed my arms, shrugged, and, with all the self-righteous confidence I could muster, said, "Well, it's not for *you*; that's why your head hurts so much."

"Amira!" my mom snapped. "That's not nice!"

The twins just stared at me. I stomped off to the next room to await my fate. My mom sighed, muttered something under her breath, and finished fixing their braids. Even from the other room, I was sure I heard the twins whispering dramatically about how "mean" I was.

After they went home, my mom pulled me aside and delivered the scolding I knew was coming. "Amira," she said, *serious mom tone* fully activated. "You can't just say things like that, even if they're true."

And there it was. The price of nice. A lesson ingrained in many of us as kids: *Being nice is more important than being real*. No matter how right you are, if it makes someone uncomfortable, you're the problem.

Looking back, I now realize I could've handled the situation differently. I loved the twins like they were my flesh and blood. Even thirty-plus years later, we're still sisters in every way that matters. If only little Amira had had the proper communication tools at her disposal. For example, I didn't know about concepts like the matching principle, which might have helped me assess the kind of conversation I was in and how to respond accordingly.

Quickly summarized, the *matching principle* explains that we typically have three types of conversations:

- **Practical conversations** focused on solving problems or making plans

- **Emotional conversations** about sharing feelings and seeking empathy

- **Social conversations** centered on connection and identity[1]

That day, I was locked into "practical" mode (I usually am—September Virgo here!): *Do you want to feel better? Your head hurts because braids aren't for you. Stop getting braids. Duh!* But the twins were experiencing an emotional conversation. They wanted empathy. And I couldn't fathom how "Poor thing, I'm sorry!" was any type of solution.

I still think I was right—even if I could/should have responded differently. But the lesson of that moment wasn't about my attitude in the face of unwitting cultural appropriation; it was about my conditioning to align with the world's expectations. It was precedent setting, the first knot in a lifetime of lessons I'd have to learn to unbraid. Their discomfort wasn't my fault, but knowing that truth isn't enough.

Maybe, like me, you've been tangled in those lessons, too. Perhaps you've been taught to swallow honesty to maintain peace. This book isn't here to coddle you or make you feel better. It's here to push you, to remind you of the child who knew the value of truth, and to help you reclaim the part of you that knew what needed to be said and done and wasn't afraid to say or do it—that is, until society coached it out of you.

Let me ask you this: Do you want to *feel* better, or do you want to *be* better? Because you can't often have both.

Can I Say Woke?

If "braid-gate" taught me about social conditioning, 2012 provided the life-altering lessons that revealed just how much that conditioning would cost. That's when I became woke—a term that, before the far right got all hot and bothered by it, used to just mean *socially and politically conscious*. Trayvon Martin's murder,[2] and the aftermath that ensued, was the pivotal moment that opened my eyes. It wasn't just another news story; it was a catalyst that transformed my understanding of the world. His death, though there had been so many before, jolted me to a level of alertness I had not previously experienced, bringing to mind questions I had not wrestled with nearly enough—questions that kept me up at night and gnawed at my sense of justice, morality, and peace.

At work the next day, Trayvon's name was on everyone's lips, the tragic details of his death igniting conversations that buzzed through the hallways. People were talking about the rallies planned in his honor. Many discussed the growing trend of wearing hoodies in solidarity—a simple, silent protest. I suppose I appreciated the gesture, but it just felt so ... superficial.

Other colleagues questioned Trayvon's actions, wondering aloud if he had "brought this on himself." I stood there, stunned, as people I admired expressed beliefs I wouldn't have imagined lurking beneath their polished, progressive exteriors. The callous disregard for the life of a seventeen-year-old boy, a child who'd simply gone to buy his little brother Skittles and iced tea, was too much. Yet, I found myself hesitating, a familiar nagging question tugging at my mind: *If I speak up, will they think I'm not nice?*

I was frustrated—with my colleagues, but also myself. I had the power and the tools to challenge those who blamed a child for his own murder, yet I stayed silent. It was the first time I considered what the price of nice was costing me. That realization set everything in motion.

I began asking the questions that plagued my mind, reexamining the beliefs I had accepted without challenge—a process that ultimately led to me writing this book. Why Trayvon? Why are people who look like me disproportionately dying? Why does this keep happening? Why don't more people see this as their fight? Why do some march in solidarity but vote against our interests? *And why, after all this time, are we still asking these same questions?*

These weren't rhetorical—they demanded answers and action. I sought out those who "got it": disruptors, thinkers, and changemakers willing to ask hard questions and endure discomfort for real answers. They didn't always look like me or share my background, but they saw the same broken systems and refused to accept them. And they led me to a difficult revelation: *Nice is not the measure.*

This truth resonates deeply with women in particular, a reflection of the ways we've been shaped by unspoken yet rigid societal expectations. Whenever I've shared it, the response has been immediate—an exhalation, a knowing *"Yaaas!"* It's not something we were explicitly taught, but something we've lived, internalized, and carried. Niceness is woven into our worth; an expectation to shrink, smooth over, and silence ourselves—even at the cost of our authenticity and brilliance.

But don't be fooled into assuming that this conditioning is limited to women. Spanning identities and generations, it's a collective expectation that substitutes niceness for connection, courage, and conviction.

More than a personal habit, it's a deeply ingrained social expectation. Dismantling it requires more than recognition; it demands transformation in how we think, feel, and act. My journey from conformity to courage, from *nice* to *nerve*, is proof of how deep and disruptive that shift can be.

Why I Fight

In 2012, I also became a mother, and suddenly, I wasn't just navigating the world for myself. I was raising a daughter in a society that would demand she "sit pretty" and "play nice." The weight of that responsibility was transformative. I knew I couldn't accept the world I'd been handed without fighting for a better one—for her, for me, for all of us.

I was quickly becoming someone I'd been taught to be terrified of: an outspoken feminist, a skeptic, a truth-teller. One of those women who were not well-behaved, who would not go quietly. One of those women I used to snicker and talk about, who I'd thought were crazy. One of those women who had the nerve to expect more. Who demanded that others live up to the values they claimed to hold. I studied and quoted James Baldwin, bell hooks, and Malcolm X, among others. Radicals. I thought often of Zora Neale Hurston's words: "If you are silent about your pain, they'll kill you and say you enjoyed it."[3]

This shift wasn't about abandoning who I was; it was about becoming who I had the potential to be. It was about living a life uninterrupted in which the cost of silence is far greater than the risk of speaking out. That's why I'm here. Not because I have all the answers, but because I've lived the questions.

This transformation didn't happen overnight. It was a slow reckoning with my own complicity in maintaining the status quo. My journey from snickering in the background to standing on the front lines was one of unlearning, confronting my fears, and accepting the discomfort of being *too much* in a world that thrives on keeping people in their place.

But breaking free from niceness isn't just personal—it's a collective responsibility. Niceness isn't harmless; it's a system of unchallenged control. It avoids confrontation and stalls progress. To dismantle its grip, we must first name it for what it is. If we're not willing to speak truth to power, then what's the fucking point?

Allow Me to Reintroduce Myself

Many of my childhood memories are rooted in the evangelical Christian church where my parents were ministers. On Sunday mornings, I was often tasked with standing at the front doors—always smiling, polite, and offering a warm handshake. The instructions for being a greeter were simple: Hand each person a program and say, *"Hello, I'm Amira, it's nice to meet you."*

That program laid out precisely what to expect during the service—when to sit, when to stand, when to sing, and how we would all engage with one another. It was a guide to making sure that everything flowed smoothly, that everyone was comfortable, and that nothing would disrupt the order of things.

Much like how I was oriented into church life, employees in corporate America are welcomed with their own kind of program—an onboarding checklist, a values statement, a cultural playbook. They're taught the spoken and unspoken rules, like what to say in meetings, how to show enthusiasm without rocking the boat, and how to fit in without standing out too much. The goal is the same: comfort, cohesion, predictability. But over time, that kind of program doesn't just shape behavior. It shapes belief. And sometimes, it asks us to trade authenticity for acceptance.[4]

Today, my operating instructions are different. Today, it's about being a force for disruption, for shaking up the systems that keep inequity alive. Not only that, but I'm ripping up the old program. Because progress is about replacing what is with what can be.

I want you to know that, in writing this, I have strived to present to you my most uninterrupted self. I am a biracial woman of Black/Chamoru heritage; a disabled, cisgender, heterosexual, Virgo, agnostic, communications executive, writer, professor, and parent. These are dimensions from which I view the world—intersections that have shaped my life and work. You will find personal stories from my life here, as well as wisdom I've gleaned from others. None of us walk this journey alone. Some content is necessarily academic in nature, and some of it is interspersed with pop culture references. Some of it is serious business, and some of it (I hope) you will find humorous. As you've already read, there will be language that some might deem unsavory. Sorry, not sorry.

This book is an open invitation to the people willing to take part with me in the uncomfortable conversations of fundamental transformation and radical reimagining—to embrace the chaos that comes from challenging entrenched systems. It's time to pierce the facade that has engendered our complacency for far too long. To those who would accept that invitation, as you move through these pages, I encourage you to rethink how you've been conditioned to engage with the world, rewrite the program, and cultivate a new greeting.

"Hello, I'm Amira—I'm here to shatter the mask of nice."

Care to join me?

INTRODUCTION

What's Wrong with Nice?!

I'm so glad you asked!

Niceness is a velvet glove over an iron fist, stifling dissent and prioritizing comfort over progress. It conditions us to accept the status quo, protecting those in power at the expense of equity and opportunity. This book deconstructs our cultural obsession with niceness, exposes its hidden costs, and offers a practical framework for moving beyond nice to create real change.

As children, we're taught that being "nice" is everything. Don't cry. Don't get angry. Don't speak up too loudly. Don't say it *that* way. And definitely don't snatch that block back from Timmy, even though he *clearly* took it from you. From the sandbox on, nice isn't just encouraged—it's enforced.

Nice is treated as a foundational virtue, a foregone conclusion regarding our behavior. And so, we rarely question it. Because we don't see it as an affliction to be remedied or, really, as any issue at all, we allow niceness to shape our lives, our relationships, and our workplaces in ways that rarely serve us. We don't examine niceness as a part of our human condition. Why would we? Somatically, niceness carries an enormous cost—not just a social or professional burden, but a deeply personal, embodied one. That is to say, it doesn't just shape how we behave; niceness shapes how we feel in our own skin, how we hold our breath, tighten our shoulders, or swallow our discomfort to maintain the illusion of calm, even when our nervous systems are screaming.[1]

It doesn't cause a scene. It doesn't demand interrogation. It just quietly settles in, training us to be agreeable instead of honest, palatable instead of powerful. But what if "nice" isn't as harmless as we think? What if it's the very thing keeping us from real progress?

Niceness is mistaken for kindness. Yes, kindness matters, but kindness is not justice—it's barely progress. Civility, too, is a hollow response to systemic harm. After all, what does civility solve when the injustice we avoid discussing is itself uncivil? Unchecked niceness is never benign. It is always, without exception, upheld because someone benefits from it, and from the toxicity that inevitably follows. If your reaction to this revelation is discomfort or defensiveness, then niceness has already done its job. It has conditioned you to protect the very systems that oppress you and others.

This reaction is by design. Sparking moral outrage distracts from systemic injustice and shields those who profit from silence and complicity. Only when we pause and ask, *"Who benefits from this niceness? Who profits from the toxicity it enables?"* can we uncover the uncomfortable truth: Those who benefit most from the system often resist change, until something within them shifts and they realize the system must, too.

Change arises from two primary drivers: force or choice.[2] Force appears direct, even inevitable, compelling action through external pressure. But the intentionality of choice fuels deliberate, lasting transformation. Choice emerges when the harm of staying the same outweighs the pain of change.[3] And yet, with niceness ingrained in our culture as the default, the recognition of that pain often comes too late—if at all. This is the cost of niceness: a reality where the discomfort of stagnation is suppressed or ignored until the damage is done, leaving us to grapple with the harm we've allowed to persist and the opportunities for progress we've let slip away.

Progress, but Make It Performative

Niceness gives the illusion of progress, but it's a mirage—devoid of substance, serving to soothe the *afflictors* rather than change reality for those *afflicted*. Consider the "great awakening" in 2020 after the world saw George Floyd murdered on video. People and organizations tripped over themselves to make personal revelations, public statements, and all manner of symbolic gestures supporting Black Lives Matter (BLM). While arguably well-intentioned, these fell short of material action or change. Examples included:

- **Corporate statements.** Many companies announced solidarity with BLM. However, few backed these gestures by changing hiring practices, addressing inequities, or supporting Black employees in tangible ways.

- **One-time donations.** Organizations made one-off donations to Black-focused causes but didn't build sustained partnerships, signaling short-term support rather than long-term commitment.

- **Book lists and movie recommendations.** People shared antiracist book and movie lists but often stopped there. Without deeper engagement—like holding difficult conversations—these efforts amounted to little.

- **Employee training sessions.** Some companies conducted antibias training but fell short of implementing implement systemic change by addressing deeper issues like leadership diversity or equitable promotion pathways.

- **Performative protests and public displays.** Participating in marches became more about optics than driving change. Returning to unchanged behaviors and environments failed to challenge inequities.

- **Hiring empty roles.** A personal favorite: Companies promoted or hired the first Black person they could find into prominent "diversity, equity, and inclusion" (DEI) roles but failed to provide appropriate structure, support, or authority for sustained change.

These actions revealed the gap between surface-level allyship and the type of commitment needed to address workplace inequities like the gender pay gap, the glass ceiling, disability discrimination, hiring biases, etc., and social inequities like racism, xenophobia, misogyny, and so much more. True allyship demands continuous, uncomfortable work that seeks to dismantle systemic injustice, challenging those closest to us and the institutions we belong to.

Wholeness in the Workplace

Performative corporate gestures may check a box, but they merely preserve the status quo. Hispanic Heritage Month or Pride celebrations may bring festive decorations to the break room, but they don't shift hiring or promotion practices. Niceness signals change without delivering it.

Corporate culture conditions us to suppress discomfort and avoid conversations that disrupt this illusion of harmony. We are expected to adhere to a "professional decorum" that separates our personal lives from our work. This unspoken requirement to compartmentalize—to keep our personal beliefs, values, and even struggles out of the workplace—lies at the heart of performative niceness in corporate spaces. The compartmentalization of our identities reinforces the illusion that harmony can be achieved by avoiding difficult topics, as though our professional and personal selves could or should exist in isolation. Yet we are not merely workers performing a role, but individuals whose lives, opinions, experiences, and identities inevitably bleed into our professional spaces. Forced separation of the personal and professional is neither natural nor sustainable—or even desirable. In fact, research by Harvard professor Amy Edmondson underscores that genuine collaboration and innovation rely on psychological safety—the belief that we can show up fully, speak honestly, and challenge norms without fear of retribution.[4] When people feel safe enough to bring their whole selves to work, they're more likely to contribute, take risks, and surface the very truths organizations need to evolve.

I believe that one of the most basic human aspirations is to be seen as our whole selves. For those of us with bills to pay, much of our waking existence is spent at a job or jobs, and we naturally want—and, increasingly, expect—our workplaces to be places where our full identities are embraced. However, this desire to show up fully and be accepted often comes into conflict with the unspoken systems within corporate culture.[5] Where niceness in the workplace is prioritized, it requires us to set aside personal convictions and act within narrow boundaries to preserve a false sense of "business as usual." In doing so, we stifle our potential for authentic connection and growth, holding back the very change we seek.

To find a recent example of the ways in which compartmentalization and "niceness," particularly in workplaces, is harmful, we need only look at the messaging surrounding the loss of Vice President Kamala Harris to Donald Trump in the 2024 presidential election. For me, and many who look like me, this election outcome wasn't simply about personality or policy preferences; it was a referendum on fundamental human rights.

That a person's humanity can be relegated to a matter of political preference is morally abhorrent. Yet, we watched in real time as a majority of voters knowingly chose a candidate whose promises and actions support authoritarianism, exclusion, and systematic harm toward marginalized groups.

In the days following the election, as the country reeled from the implications, CEOs called for "civility" and "tolerance," urging us to "move forward." Very little, if any, acknowledgment was paid to the fear and pain resulting from the profound consequences of this choice. Instead, we were expected to quiet our concerns and to simply accept an outcome that threatened to strip away the voices of and protections and freedoms for millions—a threat that has already proven to be all too real. Such calls for niceness are not about unity but about containing and minimizing discomfort, particularly for those whose lives and rights are not at immediate risk.

In the corporate world, where "professionalism" is too often synonymous with "silence," we are expected to mask our moral outrage and dissent. The demand for basic human rights is an inconvenience, a divisive issue best left undiscussed. The underlying and undeniable truth is that when civility becomes a shield for complacency, it enables structures of harm to remain intact, encouraging a passive tolerance of injustices that ultimately compromise the safety, dignity, and humanity of countless individuals. We are told to prioritize productivity over personhood, harmony over truth, and comfort over accountability. But that version of civility, one that sidesteps hard truths in favor of an artificial calm, reinforces the very systems that prevent us from achieving true justice and equality.

Today, more and more of us want to be seen not as working humans but as whole humans, people whose personal and professional lives intersect and whose work holds meaning because it reflects our values and identities. Yet true wholeness demands more than mere coexistence. In order to achieve it, we must be willing to move beyond empty rituals and disrupt the calm, swimming against the current of "niceness" that runs through our institutions. John Lewis described this as "good trouble"—deliberate, meaningful action that benefits everyone (YES, EVEN WHITE PEOPLE!) and movement toward that which we all innately desire.

The Few Who Do, the Many Who Don't

If we all want wholeness, why do so few create the disruptive change needed to make progress? Why do so many avoid it?

Consider some of the changemakers we celebrate: Martin Luther King Jr., Nelson Mandela, bell hooks, Cesar Chavez, Katherine Johnson, Greta Thunberg, Malcolm X, Malala Yousafzai, Kimberlé Crenshaw. These individuals had extraordinary talents—Dr. King's unmatched eloquence, Katherine Johnson's brilliance in mathematics—but talent alone didn't set them apart.

What truly made the difference was their courage and determination to leave behind what was comfortable for what could be. They didn't stick to the rules of doing what was "acceptable." Changemakers step out of line and disrupt the norm, not for attention, but for transformation. But they don't do it alone—their impact grows through communities, support networks, and shared visions.

People often ask me, *What can I do?* A better question might be, *What can I undo?* Small, well-meaning actions aren't enough. They never have been. Real change demands bold, intentional choices. I hope that, through this book, you'll find the inspiration to rethink what you believe, challenge what you know, and take action toward what's possible.

A Tool Kit, Not a Blueprint

To build something new, we need new tools. This book shares practices that have shaped my journey. As a communications practitioner, I start by asking: *What problem are we aiming to solve?* This clarifies our purpose and sets direction. It's followed by: *Who are we solving this problem for? Who do we need to influence, and what specific shifts in thought, emotion, or action do we want to inspire?*

To answer these questions, we investigate the motivations, values, and trusted voices of the people we wish to reach. By understanding their worldviews, we can craft messages that inspire wonder, resonate deeply, and mobilize action. Breaking down complex behavioral patterns into manageable dimensions allows us to more easily identify and replicate opportunities for prevention, intervention, restoration, or transformation.

Dimensions are the distinct yet interconnected components that shape and guide actions, decisions, and thought processes. Each dimension serves as a specific lens for understanding and addressing broader issues, offering a structured approach to analyzing, engaging with, and influencing behavior in ourselves and our institutions.

The *think-feel-do-revisit* model, rooted in social psychology, underpins the framework of this book. Using the insights and strategies it offers, we can redefine what being "nice" means, embrace the discomfort that leads to growth, inspire action, and ensure lasting, impactful change. The book is divided into four sections, one for each dimension:

Think: This section reflects on how "niceness" has been shaped by history and how it often supports unfair systems. We'll also examine how our thoughts and assumptions influence our choices and behaviors.

Feel: Here, we explore how perceptions can drive action. Through emotional awareness, we can learn to face discomfort and connect to solutions that create real change.

Do: This part focuses on taking action, highlighting habits and steps we can repeat to make a difference. It's about finding ways to take control, amplify diverse voices, and share power to challenge unfair systems.

Revisit: Change isn't a one-time thing; it's ongoing. This section reminds us to keep learning, reflect on what we've done, and improve so progress continues.

Each chapter also provides actionable steps to encourage exploration and continual improvement. Unlike rigid rules or static principles—which may imply universal applicability—these "Promising Practices" are flexible, context sensitive, and adaptive. They reflect approaches grounded in evidence, experience, and thoughtful experimentation and are designed to address specific challenges while allowing for growth and refinement. This combination ensures that strategies remain relevant, impactful, and responsive to ever-changing needs.

As Maya Angelou reminds us, "Do the best you can until you know better. Then, when you know better, do better."[6] It's about cultivating a mindset that allows you to hold yourself and others accountable in the face of complex challenges, making room for nuance as you navigate your journey. I don't want you to think of this as a checkbox exercise, after which you are granted a certificate of completion. Those kinds of prescriptive to-do lists thrive on conformity and compliance; they leave little room for audacity and feel too much like the systems I've spent much of my adult life resisting and deconstructing.

Instead, I implore you to move beyond the blueprint—a concept so central to my philosophy that I developed an entire series at my communications agency called (you guessed it) *Beyond the Blueprint*. The essence of that work, and this book, is this: You may want an outline that tells you exactly what to do, but you don't need one. Questions and nuance are inherently uncomfortable, and most people—whether consciously or not—crave the comfort of certainty. But the real value of a tool kit like the one provided here is not in rigid instructions; the real value lies in understanding and embodying a way of being that reflects the world's complexities and allows for greater adaptability, self-awareness, and purpose.

That said, while this framework is not rigid, it is also not to be taken lightly. The dimensions it explores are firm in their importance and intentionality, even as they remain adaptable to life's twists and turns. These tools will help you filter the world around you, ask better questions, engage in more honest conversations, and critique systems and behaviors with purpose.

Who This Book Is For

I can't write to everyone. It's impossible to write something that appeals and speaks directly to all people in every imaginable walk of life. Attempts to do so dilute and scatter the message, throwing everything at the wall and hoping something sticks. But I can write to those who are ready and in positions to listen and act. So, this book is primarily written with my fellow communications practitioners in mind: change agents who understand that communication—at its core—mobilizes action, shifts mindsets, and transforms systems.

People often ask me why I practice DEI within a communications role rather than at a traditional management consulting powerhouse like Deloitte, McKinsey, or BCG. To many, it seems an odd pairing, but only if they don't understand my "why." To expand people's perspectives, you must be able to frame what is possible. I firmly believe that our words shape worlds. Giving voice to something is a powerful, creative act. I once heard a communications expert from the Frameworks Institute explain that what people will do at any given moment is dictated by how they imagine the world, and how they imagine the world is shaped by the words we choose and the stories we share.

In a *New York Times* interview, James Baldwin, civil rights icon and author, expressed a similar idea: "You write in order to change the world, knowing perfectly well that you probably can't, but also knowing that literature is indispensable to the world. In some way, your aspirations and concern for a single man in fact do begin to change the world. The world changes according to the way people see it, and if you alter, even by a millimeter, the way a person looks or people look at reality, then you can change it. . . . If there is no moral question, there is no reason to write."[7]

Of course, that doesn't mean the content contained within this book is singularly applicable to professional communicators. If you're part of any workplace, you are a change agent and a communicator. If you are coaching clients, you have the opportunity to raise awareness and address impact. If you supervise others, you can be a leader in instituting change and an example of implementing effective communication in your world. If you're a vendor, a supplier, a janitor, a barista, or a stay-at-home parent, if you are simply navigating this world with empathy and respect for your fellow human, you have the power to communicate and drive change. In short, while this book isn't written *to* everyone, it can be *for* everyone.

While written through the lens of my perspective and experience, it is my sincere belief that any reader will be able to see themselves reflected in these pages and apply the content through their own lens. Ultimately, this book is for everyone who is ready to move beyond talk and surface solutions. It's for champions willing to face down the most diabolical obstacles: apathy in favor of order, self-preservation in the face of resistance, and the belief that we are powerless to make a difference. This book is not merely a critique; it's a call to action. If you are ready to stop settling for "good enough," let's work together to create something better.

Instead of paying the price of stagnation, it's time to invest in change. By embracing this book's practices, you will not only transform how you engage with the world but inspire others to do the same. We must change *our* world (ourselves, our homes, our workplaces) before we change *the* world.

And so, without further ado, I present to you *The Price of Nice.* Let's begin.

PART I
THINK

1

The
Velvet Glove
Comes Off

" It costs nothing to be nice."

What a travesty of logic!

In context, that phrase usually means "Don't be a jerk." It can be used to call out bad behavior or praise someone for basic decency. On the surface, being nice seems like an innocent, even admirable quality—a balm that soothes social interactions. But niceness often hides more profound problems. It's a learned behavior meant to keep things comfortable, avoid conflict, and preserve the existing order.

The truth is more complicated: It costs a great deal to be nice.

I'm not suggesting we throw human decency out the window; no one likes an asshole. Instead, I want us to examine niceness as a *social construct*, not a natural or inherent truth—as one of many collectively agreed-upon ideas that shape our behaviors, relationships, and institutions. You see, despite their artificial origins, social constructs carry very real consequences.[1]

That's an Invisibility Cloak!

Social constructs you may be more familiar with include race, gender roles, and the value of money. But unlike these more readily identifiable systems, niceness operates unnoticed. It exists as the default, the norm, the presumed state of acceptable behavior. More insidiously, because niceness is framed as a virtue, it is rarely scrutinized, escaping the accountability and critique it urgently requires. Instead, it becomes a cloak we gladly wrap ourselves in for the fleeting comfort of achieving acceptance.

Seemingly well-intentioned goals like "keeping the peace" and "trying to get along" obscure how niceness upholds the status quo, justifying our subconscious self-betrayal and permitting us to avoid uncomfortable truths. Like Harry Potter sneaking through Hogwarts undetected, sidestepping explicit acknowledgment of how niceness maintains compliance preserves its role as a tool for perpetuating comfort over change, appearances over authenticity, and false peace over meaningful progress.

Niceness, left unchecked, is a mechanism of control that replicates itself and reinforces the systems that thrive on its presence. In fact, precisely because it is allowed to operate without scrutiny despite the myriad ways it contributes to harm, niceness may be one of the most vicious social constructs, subtly enabling systems of oppression to persist.

It's time to name it, confront it, and demand more from ourselves and the world around us.

To chart a path forward, we must first understand how we arrived at this critical turning point. In the next few chapters, we'll build a shared foundation of terminology and concepts while uncovering the history and conditioning that have brought us to this point.

Do You Understand the Words That Are Coming Out of My Mouth?!?

Let's start with a few definitions. Everyone's experiences shape how they interpret the world and the language they use. Assuming shared understanding can lead to miscommunication, confusion, and disrupted collaboration—especially given the quirks of the English language.

Consider two terms that anchor my premise: *nice* and *nerve*. While it may not be obvious at first glance, these two familiar words actually represent starkly different approaches to navigating the world—one preserves the current norms, the other drives real change.

Nice

According to Merriam-Webster, some definitions of nice are *polite, kind; pleasing, agreeable; appropriate, fitting; well-executed.*[2] On the surface, "nice" seems downright delightful. After all, who doesn't prefer to be around polite and agreeable people? However, as I touched on briefly a moment ago, for the purposes of this book, we are not addressing nice from this defined vantage point, but as a social construct. You mustn't conflate or confuse the two. Nice—when prioritized above all else—is a trap. It can lead to

- Avoiding difficult conversations to preserve a false sense of peace

- Tolerating harmful behavior because confronting it feels uncomfortable

- Masking systemic injustices under a veneer of politeness

Nice emphasizes how things feel rather than how they are. While it soothes in the short term, it stifles growth, silences dissent, and upholds the current state of affairs in the long run.

Nerve

I propose that the opposite of "nice" is not "mean." Instead, I think of the antithesis of "nice" as "nerve." *Nerve* has a wide range of definitions, from the physical receptors in the human body that send signals to our brains to feelings of agitation or irritability (such as when someone "gets on your nerves"). We will focus on this term as it relates to *power of endurance or control; fortitude, strength; assurance, boldness; audacity.*[3]

Having nerve says "This is where I draw the line" and honors your emotional boundaries even when others don't. It's about standing firm in your beliefs and protecting your well-being or the well-being of others, even if doing so requires burning bridges. Unlike nice, which seeks to avoid discomfort, nerve leans into it, acknowledging that growth, justice, and transformation often require us to be uncomfortable—and even to make others uncomfortable. Nerve is

- Speaking up when silence feels safer

- Challenging the status quo even at the cost of relationships or personal gain

- Holding boundaries and advocating for opportunity despite criticism or misunderstanding

Nerve is about resilience and the willingness to act when it matters most. Where nice prioritizes agreeability, nerve disrupts. Choosing between nice and nerve isn't only about personal values or professional strategies. It's about the world we are building—or failing to build—for future generations.

I remind my daughter, before moments of challenge, "Get your butterflies in formation." It's my way of acknowledging that being anxious is natural, but it's also a reminder to harness that energy into action. Having the nerve to demand change is not about being fearless—it's about feeling the fear and showing up anyway. It's a call to let those fluttering butterflies guide us into the spaces that most need disruption. These small but powerful moments shape how she learns to navigate the world, with all its unspoken rules and unjust systems.

When we spread our wings, we create currents that lift others, making it easier for them to rise. The journey will be nerve-racking, but it's one we must take—individually and collectively—to inspire a future where everyone can take flight.

Words as Tools—or as Weapons

Why take the time to worry about this? Because *words matter.* Words are not passive or inert; they carry histories that shape meaning and influence how we understand the world. For example, do you know where the word "bikini" comes from? While most people associate it with two-piece swimwear, that name originates from Bikini Atoll, a Pacific island where the United States conducted tests for the atomic bomb, causing significant destruction and displacing the island's inhabitants.[4] French designer Louis Réard then took the name for his swimwear, with the idea that the revealing nature of his design was as explosive as the nuclear tests—which is its own special brand of disturbing.

Over time, the word's connection to these devastating origins has been nearly erased, replaced by images of carefree summer days at the beach. This illustrates how language can obscure deeper truths, sanitizing the legacies of harm it carries. Words mold our perceptions, frame how we understand the world, and influence what actions we believe are possible (or impossible). The stories we tell, the language we use, and even the silences we maintain form the foundation of our social, cultural, and institutional systems.

The Conditioning Matrix (Figure 1) is a visual framework I've created that reveals the layered forces that shape our default leaning toward "nice" (and discourage the boldness of "nerve"). It maps the inputs that reinforce compliance, silence, and likability on an individual, interpersonal, and institutional scale, ultimately conditioning us to value comfort over courage.

Nice is not neutral—it is often a survival strategy, a performance, a learned behavior that's been rewarded, expected, and internalized across every level of society. The Conditioning Matrix invites us to look beyond personality traits and into power structures: to question who benefits when we stay quiet, agreeable, or small. By naming these influences clearly, we gain language and awareness to challenge them. This tool is not about shame—it's about clarity. It's about recognizing the cost of niceness and reclaiming the courage of nerve as a more honest, values-driven way of being.[5] Use this matrix to interrogate your own conditioning, reflect on the roles you've been asked to play, and begin the journey of choosing alignment over approval.

The Power of Words

Words carry weight and consequences—they are never "just" words. Words drive action or inaction, their meanings evolving based on how they're used and who controls the narrative. Wielded purposefully, words can build understanding, inspire progress, and foster connection. They can heal, bringing lucidity and reconciliation. But in the wrong hands, they can manipulate and cause harm, wielded as weapons to maintain power or perpetuate injustice. That old saying, "Sticks and stones may break my bones, but words will never hurt me"? Grade-A bullshit.

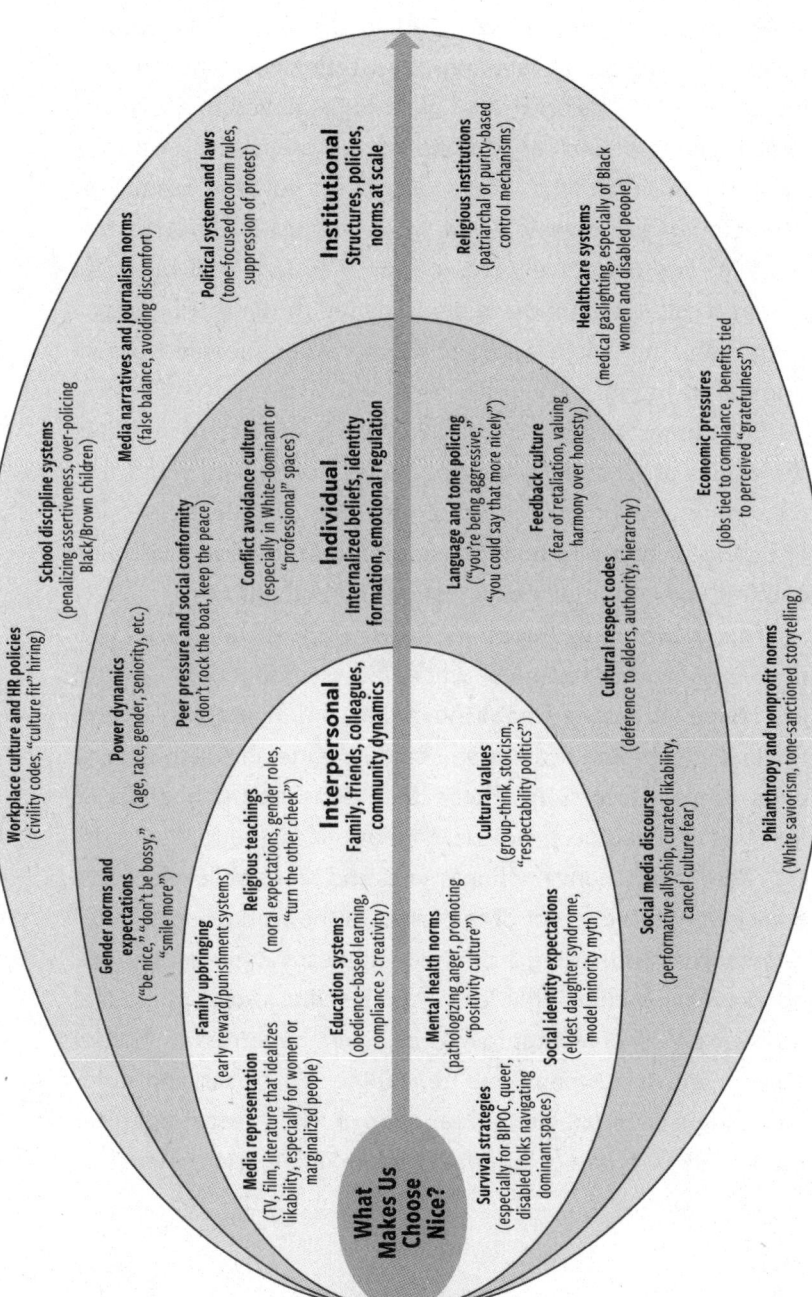

Figure 1. The Conditioning Matrix

What Makes Us Choose Nice?

Individual
Internalized beliefs, identity formation, emotional regulation

Survival strategies
(especially for BIPOC, queer, disabled folks navigating dominant spaces)

Mental health norms
(pathologizing anger, promoting "positivity culture")

Social identity expectations
(eldest daughter syndrome, model minority myth)

Social media discourse
(performative allyship, curated likability, cancel culture fear)

Interpersonal
Family, friends, colleagues, community dynamics

Media representation
(TV, film, literature that idealizes likability, especially for women or marginalized people)

Family upbringing
(early reward/punishment systems)

Education systems
(obedience-based learning, compliance > creativity)

Religious teachings
(moral expectations, gender roles, "turn the other cheek")

Cultural values
(group-think, stoicism, "respectability politics")

Cultural respect codes
(deference to elders, authority, hierarchy)

Philanthropy and nonprofit norms
(White saviorism, tone-sanctioned storytelling)

Institutional
Structures, policies, norms at scale

Gender norms and expectations
("be nice," "don't be bossy," "smile more")

Workplace culture and HR policies
(civility codes, "culture fit" hiring)

School discipline systems
(penalizing assertiveness, over-policing Black/Brown children)

Power dynamics
(age, race, gender, seniority, etc.)

Peer pressure and social conformity
(don't rock the boat, keep the peace)

Conflict avoidance culture
(especially in White-dominant or "professional" spaces)

Media narratives and journalism norms
(false balance, avoiding discomfort)

Political systems and laws
(tone-focused decorum rules, suppression of protest)

Language and tone policing
("you're being aggressive," "you could say that more nicely")

Feedback culture
(fear of retaliation, valuing harmony over honesty)

Economic pressures
(jobs tied to compliance, benefits tied to perceived "gratefulness")

Religious institutions
(patriarchal or purity-based control mechanisms)

Healthcare systems
(medical gaslighting, especially of Black women and disabled people)

We've become so accustomed to the word "nice" that it serves as a catch-all label, applied reflexively and without much thought. This erosion of meaning is linked to a psychological phenomenon called *semantic satiation*, first described by Dr. Leon Jakobovits.[6] His research on how the brain processes language revealed that when a word is repeated frequently, our cognitive connection to it fades. It becomes harder to attach emotion or significance to the word, temporarily reducing it to a series of sounds disconnected from its original meaning.

Over time, the meaning of "nice" has been shaped to reflect the values of those in power, promoting compliance and discouraging disruption. Instead of creating genuine connection or change, a focus on being nice reinforces systems that value comfort and conformity over justice and authenticity.

This is especially important in my work at the intersection of communications and DEI, where it is clear that the words we use shape outcomes. Establishing shared definitions is always the first step before strategy workshops, leadership seminars, or even simple discussions. These definitions set the boundaries for what we imagine, prioritize, and ignore.

Nice keeps conversations safe and surface-level; nerve goes straight to the root of the issue. In the workplace, a "nice" approach to addressing inequities might involve hosting feel-good events—actions that look good but don't address the real problems. A "nerve" approach, however, requires an honest assessment of company culture, calling out biases and holding leaders accountable for real change. Nice keeps organizations stuck in cycles of politeness, while nerve drives them into cycles of progress. It's more difficult, but it's the only way to move forward.

Understanding Mental Models

I'm fortunate to wear several professional hats, including the hat of a professor. One of my primary responsibilities (and greatest joys) in this role is challenging my students' thinking in creative ways to drive home meaningful lessons.

I ask students, *How would you explain building a peanut butter and jelly sandwich to someone who has never made one before?* The litany of answers I receive reveals how even common experiences vary widely based on individual perspectives. Some participants focus on technical steps, such as "Spread the peanut butter on one slice of bread and jelly on the other." Others dive into prerequisites: "Finish high school and get a job so you can afford the ingredients." Still others take a foundational approach: "Learn how to read so you can follow instructions." I've also had participants who had never even heard of a peanut butter and jelly sandwich, making it impossible for them to complete the task. While this has only happened twice, it serves as a powerful reminder of how easily we can overlook perspectives that fall outside of our own.

To add an extra layer of challenge and highlight the influence of constraints, I sometimes limit the exercise's participants by requiring that their descriptions include no more than five steps. This forces them to question assumptions they might not realize they hold—like whether everyone knows how to open a jar, select the correct type of bread, or use a knife to spread the ingredients evenly—and provides a pathway to reflect on how we unconsciously rely on mental models when navigating more complex challenges, such as those involving language or systemic influences.

Each participant's answer reflects how they see the world, their understanding of what's essential, and the steps they deem necessary to achieve a goal. The underlying mental models are deeply ingrained beliefs that operate both consciously and unconsciously to shape how we interpret reality and make decisions.[7] Like the words we use, these internal frameworks reflect societal norms, historical narratives, and personal experiences.

Here are some common mental models that you may recognize when interpreting and articulating your experiences:

CAUSE AND EFFECT

- *Belief*: "If I work hard, I will succeed."

- *How it shapes behavior*: This model drives people to prioritize effort, but it may cause them to overlook systemic barriers or external factors.

CONFIRMATION BIAS

- *Belief*: "What I already believe is true."

- *How it shapes behavior*: This model encourages people to seek information that supports their beliefs while ignoring contradictory evidence.

ZERO-SUM THINKING

- *Belief*: "If someone else wins, I lose."

- *How it shapes behavior*: This model drives competition in areas where collaboration could create mutual benefits.

LEARNED HELPLESSNESS

- *Belief*: "I can't change my situation, so I shouldn't try."

- *How it shapes behavior*: This model discourages action even when change is possible.

HIERARCHICAL THINKING

- *Belief*: "Authority figures know better than I do."

- *How it shapes behavior*: This model can lead to deference to authority even when questioning or independent
thinking is needed.

SUNK COST FALLACY

- *Belief*: "I've already invested so much, I can't stop now."

- *How it shapes behavior*: This model leads people to persist with failing projects or relationships instead of cutting their losses.

The beauty of the peanut butter and jelly metaphor is its
relatability and adaptability (aside from the two people who
had never heard of it!). Just as there is no single "correct" way
to make the sandwich, no one mental model applies univer-
sally. What's more, mental models are not fixed—they can be
shifted, expanded, or replaced. Recognizing this opens the
door to creativity, empathy, and innovation. Adjusting mental
models is not solely an intellectual exercise; it is a transformative process that empowers us to approach problems with
fresh perspectives and develop solutions that serve the collective good.

Mental models offer stability and predictability, but when
applied to complex social issues, they can also reinforce harmful
biases and inequitable outcomes. Because many people struggle to articulate (or even recognize) these models, outdated
historical or cultural influences often shape how we interact
with the world. For instance, an example of the cause and effect
mental model is the myth of meritocracy—the belief that "hard
work alone leads to success." Someone raised with this mindset

may overlook how systemic barriers like racism or sexism limit opportunities for others.

We start to see the world differently when we challenge our mental models—whether about something as simple as making a sandwich or as complex as social systems. Anyone can change their mental models; it just takes a choice to do so. By making this shift, we can break down outdated ideas and build new ones based on inclusion, fairness, and shared understanding. All that's needed are the right ingredients: curiosity, reflection, context, and a willingness to try new things. The results can feed both individuals and entire systems.

How Invisible Forces Shape Our Choices

As you read this book, I encourage you to think about the words and ideas that shape your reality. The stories we tell—and the ones we leave untold—show how subtle signals, or cues, reinforce our actions and beliefs.

How we understand an issue can drive change or keep things the same. How a message is delivered can bring people together or push them apart. Four cognitive heuristics (a.k.a. mental shortcuts) rooted in cognitive psychology and behavioral science—*anchoring, priming, framing,* and *positioning*—show how information can subtly but powerfully shape our perceptions, decisions, and actions. Let's explore these unseen influences further.

Anchoring

The peanut butter and jelly exercise provides a good example of anchoring. If the first step of your instructions is "Put peanut butter on the bread," that instruction becomes the anchor for the rest—yet it's built on unstated assumptions: the bread is out of the bag, the jar is open, and a knife is ready. If either the instruction or its underlying assumptions are incomplete or unclear, the entire process can quickly go off track.

In psychology, anchoring works in a similar way. It happens when we rely too heavily on an initial piece of information, allowing it to shape how we perceive or approach what comes next.[8] For example, seeing a high price first can make a slightly lower price seem like a bargain, even if it's still expensive.

In our American culture, "niceness" often serves as an anchor—a safe, comfortable reference point we cling to in challenging situations. It ties us to societal expectations, prioritizing harmony over hard truths and making it easier to avoid deeper, uncomfortable realities. These anchors shape how we see the world, often without our awareness, subtly discouraging growth and change.

Recognizing the anchors requires introspection and the courage to confront uncomfortable truths. As college professor and activist Toni Cade Bambara famously asked, "What are you pretending not to know today?"[9] Similarly, awareness of anchoring incites us to ask, "What assumptions have I made that are influencing how I see or solve this?" By identifying the reference points that shape our perceptions, we can challenge limiting beliefs and move toward greater authenticity and understanding.

Priming

Priming is a communication tool closely tied to anchoring. It involves preparing people to think or act in a certain way through subtle cues or stimuli. While anchoring connects behaviors to specific ideas or symbolic cues, priming exposes individuals to certain emotions, words, or images that influence their reactions.[10]

Have you ever seen *The Truman Show*? In the movie, the main character, Truman Burbank, has unknowingly lived his entire life inside the completely fabricated town of Seahaven as a part of a reality TV show. Everyone he interacts with, including his family and friends, is an actor. Everything around him is a facade. In order for Truman to accept his life as normal and idyllic, he has been primed to discourage curiosity and not to seek experiences outside of his environment. He is constantly exposed to cues reinforcing the feeling that his world is safe and that the world beyond contains only heartbreak. The show's writers even killed off his father's character in a tragic boating accident when Truman was a child to discourage him from wanting to travel. This trauma was then continually reinforced by "news stories" of other tragedies, all meant to make sure he stays in his place.

While this Hollywood tale may seem extreme, priming works the same way in our lives, quietly shaping perceptions and behaviors, creating a powerful, self-reinforcing narrative that traps us in compliance. It is only when Truman begins to notice the inconsistencies in his environment that he starts to challenge the narrative and seek the truth, ultimately gathering the nerve to break free from his constructed reality. Similarly, once we recognize the systems meant to keep us in our place, we must summon the courage to disrupt those ingrained patterns.

In a corporate setting, priming can occur through the physical environment and organizational language. For example, an office that prominently displays motivational posters with phrases like "There's no 'I' in 'team'," or "Harmony equals success" primes employees to prioritize collaboration and avoid actions perceived as disruptive. Likewise, during meetings, if leaders repeatedly emphasize "staying aligned" or "gaining consensus," employees may feel subtle pressure to avoid expressing dissenting opinions, even when constructive feedback could drive innovation and lead to better outcomes.

Awareness of priming forces us to ask, "When am I choosing nice over nerve?" This question encourages introspection about the subtle cues and societal expectations that steer us. Recognizing these influences allows us to challenge the default behaviors that priming encourages and instead choose nerve.

Framing

Framing involves deciding what to emphasize and how to set the context for an experience, shaping how people perceive and respond to it.[11] It's a powerful communication tool that dictates how stories are told, ideas are presented, and actions are judged.

To that point, consider how a subtle change in framing makes a massive difference in how the message of the following two sentences is received:

I don't like racism, but this looting has got to stop.

I don't like this looting, but the racism has got to stop.

The way these sentences work grammatically, what is said before the comma is diminished, and what is said after becomes the priority. The first one, while not condoning racism, gives prominence to maintaining order. The second, while not condoning property destruction, gives top billing to addressing the underlying cause: a reaction to centuries of systemic oppression. Think about this in the context of how you may have received coverage of something like the Black Lives Matter protests, for example.

Do you remember Colin Kaepernick? In a 2016 preseason game Kaepernick, then an NFL quarterback for the San Francisco 49ers, was shown on camera sitting down during the national anthem. When asked why he had not stood with his teammates, he explained that it was to protest police brutality and racial inequality. However, despite his expressly stated intentions, certain media outlets framed the act as unpatriotic and disrespectful toward the US flag and military. Looking to refocus the discourse, Kaepernick sought the advice of a former NFL player who had previously served in the Army and decided to kneel rather than sit during the anthem in future games, to indicate his respect for military personnel—but to no avail.[12] The media's framing was set, and at the end of the season his football career effectively ended.

Framing plays a significant role in how we experience and interpret the world. It shapes public perception and discourse and can either amplify or distort the intent of words and actions. In Kaepernick's case, for many it was easier to try to change the narrative, to dismiss his actions as "un-American," than to face uncomfortable truths and engage in difficult conversations about racial injustice and inequality. In the same way, the framing of niceness as a universal virtue that begets acceptance or status discourages critical examination of its less obvious implications, leaving little room to question how it upholds inequities or stifles authentic connections.

Recognizing when these systems are in play helps us to critically engage with the world around us, allowing us to reframe it in ways that promote genuine understanding and progress. Awareness of framing invites reflection on how our language impacts both our present and our future and pushes us to ask, "How do my words define the reality I live in and the reality I hope to create?" It also focuses our attention on which narratives we emphasize and which we may leave out, shaping our perceptions, experiences, and possibilities.

Positioning

Positioning is a behavioral communication tool that strategically shapes how ideas, individuals, or actions are perceived.

Framing highlights specific aspects of a story to shape perception, while positioning defines the broader role or significance of an idea, individual, or action within a larger context. It determines where something stands relative to everything else, affecting how people value or respond to it. Unlike anchoring and priming, which link behavior to specific cues, positioning works alongside framing to establish overall context and meaning.[13]

To use our previous example, the media positioned Kaepernick as an outsider to American values, calling him unpatriotic and disruptive. This positioning placed him in direct opposition to the perceived ideals of the NFL and its audience, reinforcing a narrative that cast him as a divisive figure rather than a champion for justice. As a result, he was blackballed from the league, further solidifying his role as an antagonist in the larger cultural debate.

Taylor Swift is another striking example of how positioning works within the broader culture. I'll be careful here, lest I risk raising the ire and provoking the wrath of the "Swifties," but I think it's fair to say that, for much of her early career, she was positioned as America's sweetheart. Her carefully curated image emphasized relatability, charm, and an apolitical stance that kept her appealing to broad audiences as she transitioned from teenage country music star to pop icon. However, this positioning began to shift as Swift confronted various challenges.

As a public figure with a massive following, Swift has faced criticism in the past for remaining silent on pressing issues like abortion rights, LGBTQIA+ advocacy, Black Lives Matter, and other causes. Her reluctance to speak out was interpreted as avoiding controversy to protect her image. But in recent years she has increasingly repositioned herself, using her platform to advocate for marginalized communities and even taking a definitive stance politically. While this decision alienated some fans and drew ridicule from conservative outlets, it redefined her position as an artist willing to disrupt the status quo for her values.

A similar pivotal moment occurred during her public battle with industry executive Scooter Braun over the ownership of her music catalog.[14] Swift's decision to fight for her rights and openly discuss the exploitation of women in the music industry marked a bold departure from her "nice" persona. But instead of being celebrated for standing up for herself and others, she was labeled emotional, difficult, and even vengeful by many media outlets—classic criticisms aimed at women who assert their nerve in male-dominated industries.

(It's important to note that Taylor Swift's journey is shaped by privileges that most people don't have—privileges that give her the platform and resources to handle backlash and take bold stances. This context matters because it highlights how power dynamics lower the risks for some when making these transitions.)

Awareness of positioning encourages us to ask, "Who might I become if I were free from the undue influence of nice?" This question explores how the societal expectation of niceness shapes our identity and pushes us into a specific role. It invites us to imagine a different position for ourselves—one where we are not defined by the constraints of nice but by our own values and potential.

Swift's evolution highlights the complexities of shifting our assigned roles. Nice is positioned as the "safe" or "correct" approach, avoiding disruption, discomfort, or backlash and maintaining harmony and social approval. In contrast, nerve is frequently positioned as risky, disruptive, and even controversial, challenging the boundaries of what society deems acceptable. However, Swift's journey illustrates that positioning is not only about public perception, but also about aligning one's actions with purpose.

In both personal and professional contexts, moving from nice to nerve requires intentional positioning: shifting from what feels safe to what feels true, regardless of the risks. By embracing this shift, we redefine not only how others see us but also how we see ourselves. If we position nice as the ideal, we reinforce behaviors that prioritize comfort over growth. On the other hand, if we position nerve as a courageous and necessary force for change, we empower ourselves and others to challenge norms, confront discomfort, and push for transformation.

Centering the Margins for Collective Good

There is a foundational mental model we must keep in mind: *When we solve for those most at the margins, we solve for everyone.* Inspired by a lecture by American lawyer and activist Mari Matsuda,[15] it is at the core of my work and worldview. Matsuda affirms that centering the most marginalized is the path to collective progress. That's why change must begin at the edges, by elevating those most often overlooked, and ripple inward to transform the whole—because the most marginalized hold the truths and needs that should shape the center.

What does this look like? Malcolm X once famously stated that Black women are the most disrespected, unprotected, and neglected people in society.[16] Nothing in my experience has led me to believe that this observation does not ring true to this day. So, given that understanding, when we work to meet the needs of Black women, for example, we create change that ripples outward, empowering entire communities and creating a better world for everyone. Of course (I feel compelled to clarify), this concept is not exclusive to Black women, but will change depending on the context. Lord knows there's enough discrimination to go around.

Some will undoubtedly resist this idea, misbelieving that focusing on *any* marginalized population means disregarding everyone else. Nothing could be further from the truth. The push for change is not about exclusion or taking resources away from others. This is not a matter of "affirmative action," but rather takes inspiration from nature. In a forest ecosystem, trees are connected through shared roots. Older, stronger, more established trees will redirect resources to support younger, growing trees or those in need, thereby nurturing the whole forest. Similarly, when we center the needs of those who are often overlooked or underserved, we cultivate an environment that strengthens everyone, improving resilience and well-being across the board.

PROMISING PRACTICE 1
Change Your Mind before You Change the System

The stories throughout this chapter explore some of the forces that shape our perceptions: anchoring, priming, framing, and positioning. This tool will help you challenge those forces and shift your perspective.[17]

Steps to Give Your Mental Models a Makeover

Check yo' self (anchoring)
In the peanut butter and jelly exercise, you experienced how your first step anchored the process—assumptions shaped the outcome. Similarly, the first information we encounter often defines our perspective. To challenge this, question your starting point. Ask yourself:

- Why do I believe this?

- Is this belief rooted in evidence or outdated norms?
- What might change if I reconsidered my starting point?

Example: If you believe leadership must be confident and assertive, consider how this belief was shaped. Could collaborative or introverted styles also succeed?

Borrow someone else's glasses (*priming*)

In *The Truman Show*, Truman's world was filled with cues to keep him in place. What cues have shaped your perspective? To disrupt them, seek new viewpoints and step into someone else's experience. Ask yourself:

- What perspectives might challenge my assumptions?
- How have I been shaped to see this situation in a certain way?
- How can I invite others' insights?

Example: If you assume remote work hinders productivity, ask a thriving remote colleague for their perspective. What insights could shift your view?

Flip the script (*framing*)

Colin Kaepernick's protest was reframed to focus on patriotism, not racial injustice, altering public perception. Framing defines focus—reframing changes outcomes. Ask yourself:

- What happens when I shift the focus?
- How does reframing alter the response?
- What can I learn by trying a new approach?

(CONTINUED)

Example: If your team defaults to consensus-driven decisions, try empowering individuals to make specific calls. Notice how it shifts dynamics and outcomes.

Zoom out, babe *(positioning)*

Taylor Swift's evolution from "America's sweetheart" to bold advocate shows how positioning shapes identity. Similarly, niceness is positioned as "safe," reinforcing comfort over courage. Zooming out reveals systemic influences and new possibilities. Ask yourself:

- How does this connect to larger systems?
- What shifts when I focus on the system, not the person?
- What new opportunities emerge from a broader view?

Example: Instead of blaming a colleague for avoiding conflict, consider how your workplace positions "niceness" as a virtue. How could reframing this culture create space for authenticity?

Before We Move Forward, We Go Back

Understanding these underlying constructs is essential for creating the change we all deserve. Words matter. Without a common understanding of terms, transformation efforts often fail. Recognizing the systems at work around and within you is the first step toward progress. Each following chapter will build on this groundwork, challenging you to embrace the courage needed. It's not easy, but it is necessary.

Having established that, what we're gonna do is go back, way back, back into time . . .

2
Nice by Design

Before dismantling something, we must understand how it came to be. From childhood, we're taught to be nice—play fair, share, say *please* and *thank you*. As we grow, niceness becomes a rule, a prerequisite for success and belonging in schools, workplaces, and society. Before we grasp the concept, we stand in classrooms pledging our fealty to one nation, under God. But beneath this civility lies a tool of control, a product of historical and systemic conditioning.[1]

This chapter traces the historical roots of America's fixation on niceness, even when it hinders justice and equity. Born from colonial conformity and shaped by powerful institutions, this legacy persists today.[2] In Chapter 3, we'll dive deeper into psychology and sociology, but for now, one key concept—psychological projection—helps explain why many Americans resist confronting our past. Understanding this will frame the insights ahead.

Simply stated, many Americans avoid confronting the hard truths of our history because they're uncomfortable—too dark, too raw. Some White parents don't want their children to learn about the grim reality of slavery and potentially face the complicity of their ancestors. It's too unsettling, they say. Too disruptive. So they ban books. DEI initiatives explain truths about how the playing field has never been level and reveal how systems of oppression didn't end with Jim Crow laws but still exist today.[3] So they invent terms like "reverse racism" and do their best to dismantle these programs. But avoiding these truths doesn't make them go away.

Psychological projection happens when people blame others for their own discomfort. For example, conservatives often criticize liberals for going to college, calling them elitist and out of touch. Why? Studies indicate that conservatism is often linked to cognitive shortcuts– patterns of thinking that favor simplicity over introspection, avoidance over disruption, and complacency over justice.[4] Because higher education teaches critical thinking and fosters openness to change, it challenges ingrained beliefs and reveals deep-seated insecurities. Research supports this, showing that emotional intelligence and self-awareness are more strongly associated with left-leaning ideologies. It takes courage to ask questions, be introspective, and open yourself to the possibility that you've been wrong. Belittling others for doing what you are unwilling to do is just easier.

It doesn't have to be this way, though. Research shows there is a path to bridging ideological divides, and it's not paved with more facts or louder arguments. A 2024 study published in the *Journal of Applied Psychology* found that people are more willing to trust ideological opponents when those opponents speak from personal experience rather than citing statistics or generalized stories.[5] The authors call these stories that expose the speaker's own vulnerability or hardship "self-revealing personal narratives," and they report that they consistently foster trust, even in discussions of contentious issues such as abortion or the minimum wage. In other words, what we often label as "laziness" in our ideological opponents may, in fact, be fear—fear of being wrong, of being judged, of confronting truths that make comfort untenable. This research underscores that vulnerability, not volume, is the currency of trust. When people disclose something humbling or difficult, they signal honesty, and that signal is harder to dismiss than a fact sheet or a fiery speech. And while this kind of storytelling may feel risky, it's far more effective at opening minds and building bridges than shaming or stereotyping ever will be.

This understanding isn't new. *The Authoritarian Personality*, written by Theodor W. Adorno et al. in 1950, explored how people with rigid beliefs, no matter their level of education, often resist seeing other perspectives that challenge their worldview. My goal in explaining psychological projection isn't to categorize right-leaning people as intellectually lazy. I grew up in a Republican household, and I've had to contend with my own tendencies and patterns of thought that no longer serve me. I share this because I've seen, in myself and others, the reward of doing the hard thing.

And I certainly don't mean to romanticize a right-versus-left dynamic. There's a conversation to be had at another time about how our two-party political system has failed us. Us versus them has rarely accomplished any good. But the longer we avoid discomfort, whether on a personal level or within our institutions, the more deeply entrenched our problems become, and we keep reinforcing old systems even when those systems are unfair. In the United States, institutions were built to protect power for specific groups. We still see these patterns in our elections, schools, and criminal justice system. The discomfort of confronting the truth won't last forever—but the growth and transformation it sparks can create lasting impact. Finding the courage is the first step toward building something new.

With that in mind, let's continue our journey and dig into the historical context in which America became conditioned to comply.

Colonial Civility and Social Survival

Early settlers, particularly the Puritans, brought to the colonies a strict sense of social conformity rooted in religious and moral doctrine.[6] In isolated communities where survival depended on cooperation, niceness wasn't just a virtue—it was a form of social currency. The Puritan ethic emphasized humility, deference, and outward displays of morality as essential for maintaining social order. To survive together, people learned to keep the peace, suppressing their discomfort, fears, and critiques to maintain a harmonious facade.

Those who failed to adhere to the collective expectation of civility faced harsh consequences. Dissent was met with public shaming, physical punishment, or even banishment. To disrupt the fragile peace or step beyond the bounds of convention was not just a social risk; it was a threat to one's very survival. For those of you who may have read the book in school (or watched the movie the night before the book report was due), think along the lines of *The Scarlet Letter* by Nathaniel Hawthorne.

Perhaps one of the most straightforward, if not the most familiar, historical examples is the story of Roger Williams, a visionary whose groundbreaking ideas challenged the rigid norms of his time.[7] Williams was a staunch advocate for religious freedom and was the first to call for the separation of church and state. He also strongly defended Indigenous people's rights, arguing that colonists should purchase land directly from the Indigenous population rather than claiming it through royal charters. His beliefs, including questioning the Massachusetts

Bay Colony's land titles and advocating for equitable treatment of Indigenous peoples, led to his banishment in 1636.

Williams went on to found the settlement of Providence in what would become Rhode Island. There, he established fair dealings with Indigenous tribes such as the Narragansett, setting a precedent for justice in land ownership by paying them for the land he settled on. The principle of church–state separation would go on to influence founding father Thomas Jefferson and even find its way into the United States Constitution as a part of the First Amendment in the Bill of Rights.

Looking back, one might assume that Williams's impact on history would highlight the benefits of thinking outside the box. But alas, it is instead one of many stories that highlights how American culture was founded on a legacy of required conformity. In a world where niceness was necessary for survival, authenticity became a liability, and those who asked questions or deviated from social norms were deemed unworthy of inclusion. Individuals who expressed dissatisfaction or defiance— or even, dare I say, engaged in rebellion—were considered a danger to civilized society. For a nation that exists because of revolution, that's pretty ironic, don't you think?

Manifest Destiny and the Facade of White Civility

The invention of Whiteness itself stems from this kind of conformity. If you stop to think about it, the settlers that came to the "New World" would not have identified themselves as "White" people.[8] They would have identified with their national heritage (English, Irish, Italian, Dutch, French), or perhaps a religious designation (Puritan, Quaker, Protestant, Catholic).[9] The need to define themselves as "White" only came about once they felt it necessary to distinguish themselves from the "other": the "White" man versus the "red" or "Black," the "civilized" versus the "savages," *people* versus those considered subhuman—terms that expose how language was weaponized to justify hierarchy and harm. And so, the construct of Whiteness came into existence as a means to set one group above the rest.

As the nation expanded westward under the banner of Manifest Destiny,[10] White settlers and politicians framed their colonial expansion as a noble and civilizing mission. Believing themselves divinely destined, even mandated, by God to expand across the North American continent, the displacement and genocide of Indigenous peoples were justified through a lens of civility and moral superiority.[11] And so, niceness became a shield for violent conquest.

Acts of violence, theft, and forced assimilation were carried out under the guise of benevolence. Settlers maintained an image of politeness and righteousness even as they participated in untold brutality. We see this in the sanitized imagery that permeates American culture to this day—even our holiday celebrations.[12] The myth of Thanksgiving was created in the hopes of healing the rift caused by the Civil War. The lie of the harmonious gathering of Puritans and Indigenous peoples sitting side by side, breaking bread and exchanging smiles, has been perpetuated for generations, masking the reality of violence, betrayal, and systemic erasure.

This colonial dynamic is not unique to America. Indeed, the English, French, Dutch, Spanish, and others have utilized similar principles in their conquests around the world. But no matter who the colonizers are, these actions operate based on a dangerous precedent: that one can engage in or benefit from oppression while maintaining the appearance of moral decency. As long as individuals upheld the surface-level behaviors of civility—politeness, decorum, and avoidance of conflict—they could justify or ignore the violence underlying their actions. Niceness became a performance of sorts, a way to maintain the illusion of goodness while preserving unjust systems.

This pattern of White civility laid the groundwork for how future generations would navigate issues of race, class, and power. You can track this throughout American history: from the displacement of the Indigenous peoples, to slavery, to Reconstruction, to Jim Crow laws, to redlining, to the war on drugs and mass incarceration. Instead of confronting the realities of systemic harm, niceness became a way to sidestep discomfort and maintain the existing order. This historical conditioning taught Americans that keeping the peace, even a false peace, was preferable to reckoning with injustice.

Post-War America and the Cult of Conformity

In the aftermath of World War II, having saved the world from Adolf Hitler and the authoritarian fascism of the Nazi party (even if temporarily?), the torch of American liberty seemed to burn brighter than ever.[13] The so-called "American Dream" painted a picture of suburban bliss, prosperity, and social order. The 1950s' ideal of the nuclear family—with its neatly manicured lawns and gendered roles—reinforced niceness as a moral virtue and conformity as a core American value that held the keys to success and acceptance.

But consider the underlying systems that make up the backdrop of this blissful picture. The portraits of the idyllic Main Street in Jim Crow America would have featured signs marked "Whites only."[14] White soldiers returned from war to raucous fanfare, generous educational benefits, and financial bonuses that enabled them to purchase homes, buy property, and start businesses.[15] Black men, having fought in the same war, were not afforded the same benefits.[16] Denied bank loans for homes and businesses, they were forced to live on "the other side of the tracks," working menial blue-collar jobs while their children attended segregated schools—all so that the images of the ideal American homes, with their picket fences, milkmen making their deliveries, and children playing in the streets, would not include any Black faces.[17]

To challenge these norms was to risk being labeled as unpatriotic. This cult of conformity bred a fear of conflict, making niceness not just a preference but a survival strategy. Protests—even peaceful protests, like lunch counter sit-ins—were not to be tolerated. This prevailing narrative wasn't just about suppressing dissent, but about upholding a national illusion of unity, prosperity, and moral righteousness.

Sugar and Spice and Everything Nice

"Have you spanked your wife today?" It's not just some provocative question or misguided attempt at humor (and certainly not any type of sexual innuendo, as might be inferred by modern standards). It's a chilling reflection of 1950s America's cultural positioning, presented to adults through mainstream advertisements as a legitimate form of behavioral correction.[18] Such messages normalized—and even encouraged—the belief that intimate physical violence was an acceptable and necessary solution for women who dared step out of line, serving as a not-so-subtle threat to stay in their place.

These endorsements were not anomalies, but rather reflections of a society deeply invested in controlling women's behavior, entrenching a legacy of domestic violence that continues to echo in our societal norms today. By framing abuse as a form of care or correction, they justified the suppression of women's voices, reinforcing a hierarchy where a woman's primary role was subservience.

Throughout the millennia, women, more than any other group, have been subjected to the "tyranny of niceness."[19] Of course, this is compounded exponentially when you factor in different facets of identity, such as race. This expectation of niceness has been wielded to suppress autonomy, enforce conformity, and perpetuate systemic inequities under the guise of civility and moral virtue—sometimes in ways you may not have previously thought about.

Consider with me, if you will, the humble bicycle. A seemingly uncontroversial invention, bicycles became a powerful tool for women to reclaim mobility and agency in a world that demanded their docility, allowing them unprecedented freedom to travel unchaperoned.[20] Challenging the rigid norms of the late 19th and early 20th centuries, riding a bicycle was seen as a rebellion against the decorum expected of women, making it a potent symbol of physical liberation—a literal and symbolic act of movement away from societal constraints and toward self-determination. Women daring to ride a bicycle were even seen as morally suspect—some critics going so far as to suggest it was a gateway to sex work (seriously, WTF!?).

This disdain was not solely a referendum on newfound freedom, but was tied to another "scandal." Riding bicycles required women to wear practical clothing such as bloomers or even (*gasp*) pants, which were viewed as indecent and masculine compared to the restrictive skirts and corsets society demanded. Of course, the backlash was not merely about propriety or the fashion revolution of ladies' trousers; it was about power and those who sought to maintain it.

World War II also marked a pivotal moment in the socialization of women.[21] As men were drafted into military service, millions of women entered the workforce to fill roles traditionally reserved for men. From factory floors to administrative offices to baseball fields, women demonstrated their capabilities and gained a new sense of purpose and financial independence. You may be familiar with Rosie the Riveter, with her red bandana and flexing bicep; her image became an iconic symbol of this era, representing women's contributions to the war effort at home.

But when the war ended, roles again shifted. In an abrupt about-face, women were expected to make way for the returning male veterans and resume their domestic roles. For many, this transition was not voluntary or welcome. They had tasted independence and ambition, redefining what "women's work" could be, only to be forced back into conformity and back into the kitchen. This pattern of utilizing women's labor during crises only to then discard their contributions afterward entrenched the notion that women's desires and ambitions were secondary to societal needs. Further, their standing depended on their alignment with and subservience to men.

A seismic shift in gender dynamics occurred in 1960, however, when birth control in the form of a pill was approved in the United States. This marked the first time that women had ever had a reliable means to plan their families and careers, granting them a measure of control over their bodies and futures that had previously been denied. This innovation enabled women to pursue higher education and professional opportunities, disrupting the traditional expectations of early marriage and constant childbearing. Yet, as you might imagine, this liberation was fraught with judgment. Women who chose to use birth control were labeled promiscuous or selfish, reinforcing the idea that their agency was a threat to societal norms.

Progress over the years has been slow and hard-won. For example, although the Nineteenth Amendment to the US Constitution was ratified in 1920, stating that it was unconstitutional to deny women the right to vote based on sex, it was not until the Voting Rights Act was passed in 1965 that poll taxes, literacy laws, and other barriers preventing women (especially Black, Indigenous, Latina, Asian, and other women who face compounded marginalization) from voting were actually removed. You may have noticed that the fight continues to this day. When the Supreme Court overturned *Roe v. Wade* in 2022, it marked the end of 50 years of protection for women's autonomy when it comes to medical choices about our bodies. It also opened the door to other fundamental freedoms being challenged, such as the right to contraception, threatening to reverse our already tenuous progress.

From the domestic sphere to public spaces, women have been conditioned to make themselves small and unthreatening in a world that prioritizes male dominance and comfort, placing others' needs and expectations over their desires and ambitions. This conditioning is not incidental but intentional, maintaining a patriarchy where women's empowerment is seen as disruptive rather than necessary. This reminds us that niceness has never been benign—it has always been a tool of control.[22]

Do unto Others ... Whether They Want You to or Not!

Perhaps second only to notorious enslaver Thomas Jefferson penning the words "all men are created equal," one of the greatest American ironies is the way that religion—especially one claiming to follow the teachings of a figure who emphasized sacrifice and preached about lifting up those occupying the margins of society—has been used to facilitate systems of power and oppression. The American evangelical church has profoundly shaped our country's behavior, values, and cultural norms, impacting legal systems, social customs, and education.

The pervasive reach of Christianity in the United States has woven itself into the nation's very fabric, even for those who do not actively practice the faith or claim a religious identity. This influence is so deeply embedded that it often goes unnoticed. Yet, it guides our expectations of ourselves and others, defining what it means to be good, righteous, and worthy of respect.

This intertwining of Christian values with American identity is presented as a pathway to divine favor and moral superiority. The framework of collective acquiescence, presented as God's will, seeks certainty, discourages confrontation, fosters conformity, and elevates docility as a sign of spiritual strength. To fall outside of what is viewed as acceptable by the "moral majority" is painted as sinful, even risking eternal damnation. This distorted interpretation of scripture—effectively, moral blackmail—has nothing to do with serving your fellow man (or even serving God), but in fact maintains inequitable power dynamics. It has been particularly weaponized against marginalized groups and has been used to justify any number of moral atrocities, including slavery and the subjugation of women, by encouraging individuals to suppress their grievances, mute their dissatisfaction, and prioritize harmony, even in the face of harm or injustice. If my upbringing in Christian ministry has shown me anything, it's that within the church, you will often find both a Bible and a whip—tools for salvation and submission wielded side by side.

Interestingly, to illustrate how this works, we only have to look as far as the New Testament. In the stories of Jesus, as described in the Bible, though the Roman Empire controlled the government, much of life for the Jews was presided over by the religious establishment. While Jesus adhered to their laws and even taught in their temples, he also regularly challenged the Pharisees (the religious leaders) directly. Turning over tables in a temple marketplace and calling them out publicly, his actions threatened the authority and control of the establishment.

Meanwhile, Jesus's following grew even as he chose to spend his time with those the church frowned upon and focused his teachings on helping the poor. Indeed, Jesus was so disruptive that the Pharisees conspired with the Roman government to have him killed.

The dominant role of Christianity in American culture cannot be understated. This pervasive influence has created a landscape where niceness is not just a cultural expectation but a deeply ingrained requirement of righteousness. This conditioning reinforces systemic inequities, discourages resistance, and leaves individuals grappling with the internal conflict between moral conformity and the pursuit of justice. To fully understand the roots of niceness in our country, we have to acknowledge how deeply these "Christian" ideals are embedded in our collective psyche and the ways in which the church has betrayed its core teachings to align itself to structures of power. Given that they are supposed to follow Jesus's example, you would think that these church folk would know better. I don't know about you, but when I attended Sunday school, I was taught that the Pharisees were the bad guys in the story.

Kids These Days...

This American legacy has been passed down from generation to generation, but experienced in drastically different ways. Given that I've already highlighted some of the historical context affecting the Boomers, let's talk about my generation (Millennials) and those who came right before (Gen X). The problem? The same structures of power exist, the same desire for adherence to social norms remains pervasive, and the same conditioning conspires to keep us quiet, compliant, and stuck in a world we didn't design, navigating systems we'd rather burn to the ground.

American History X

As Generation X (born mid-1960s to early 1980s) hit the scene, the solid ground of American certainty began to shift. The oldest of this generation were toddlers when Martin Luther King Jr. was assassinated and in preschool for the moon landing. It was the end of the "free love" hippy movement and the beginning of the disco era rebellion against the mainstream. They experienced the oil crisis, the premiere of the *Star Wars* movie, the Cold War, the birth of hip hop, and Reaganomics.

But perhaps most significantly, this generation spent their childhood and formative years in the shadow of the Vietnam War. In World Wars I and II, it was very clear who the bad guys were and very easy for people to get on board with America's role in those conflicts. Victory in those wars meant that Americans could wrap themselves in the flag, secure in their country's position as a military superpower and a global beacon of moral superiority. The Vietnam War was the first in American history that we undeniably lost—a moment that shattered the nation's veneer of certainty and invincibility. More than that, it was the first war where people questioned if we should have even been fighting in the first place.

Generation Why?

Then came the Millennials (born early 1980s to mid-1990s), and everyone got a trophy. We grew up with Barney, big-haired rock bands, MTV, *Saved by the Bell*, and *TGIF*, not to mention the touchstone cultural controversies of Tupac versus Biggie, NSYNC versus the Backstreet Boys, Letterman versus Leno, and *Friends* versus *Seinfeld*. The Gulf War ensued, Congress wanted to censor our music, the mystique of the Oval Office was sullied by a little blue dress, and Al Gore invented the internet.

Suddenly, you didn't need bookshelves full of the *Encyclopedia Britannica* to access the world's information. Computers were in our homes, and phones were in our pockets. Along came Y2K, 9/11, the endless war in Afghanistan, and the ill-founded war in Iraq. We witnessed the flailing of news media and the rise of social media. Then, the financial collapse of 2008. Student debt skyrocketed, job prospects nosedived, and we watched in real time as the American Dream crumbled at our feet.

(I would like to send a special shout-out to the "X-ennials." Members of this micro-generation (1977–1983) were born with one foot in two very different worlds. Experiencing an analog childhood and a digital adulthood, this group of people were the first to have a Nintendo. They are young enough to operate a smartphone, but old enough to not quite understand how Instagram works.)

Truth, Justice, and the American Way

Where Gen X saw the first cracks in the American facade, Millennials experienced a chasm. The certainty and conformity prized by the Boomers became less and less our concern, and their vision of America seemed like more of a myth than Superman. Despite the many technological advancements of the late 20th and early 21st centuries, hope diminished—and no amount of Danny Tanner dad talks would be able to solve all our problems. Issues like climate change, persistent inequalities, and economic instability have made us question, for the first time, whether the generations to come will actually be worse off than we were.

Our priorities have shifted. People are having fewer children. We want to work to live, not live to work (if we even want to go into the office at all). Rising housing prices and interest rates mean that even basic aspirations like home ownership are becoming less and less a part of our reality. And algorithms have conspired to ensure that we are at once more connected and more divided than ever.

Naturally, this shift into uncertainty has engendered both fear and a determination to swing the pendulum back the other way. Witness the rise of the "Make America Great Again" movement. While Donald Trump may be the face of this contingency, what lurks behind is a desperate desire to cling to power. Just look at the MAGA talking points: education "reform," stripping away women's rights and a return to gendered roles, vilifying immigrants and backlash against diversity initiatives, demonizing the LGBTQIA+ community and other marginalized groups, and an emphasis on American strength. Basically, the denouncing of anything that doesn't fit into the picture of the "Whites only," yard-with-a-picket-fence 1950s ideal.

History's Grip—Why Context Matters

The old saying "If we don't learn from history, we're bound to repeat it" rings especially true today. Book bans and efforts to erase history from US schools aren't new; they're longstanding tools of control. Margaret Mead said, "Never doubt that a small group of thoughtful, committed citizens can change the world."[23] But just as small groups can drive progress, they can also set us back. Indeed, a 2023 *Washington Post* study found that just 11 people were behind 60 percent of book challenges in the previous school year, shaping what children learn and distorting history.[24]

History equips us to challenge efforts to erase truth and build a better future. Today's patterns echo the past, where keeping the peace often trumped real change. What seem like individual choices are shaped by deeper cultural and political forces. Recognizing this helps us uncover biases and create solutions that disrupt unjust systems.

History shows us that we have the power to make change. By learning from the past, we can rewrite the rules and build a future where fairness and justice matter more than just being polite. True progress comes from understanding the hard truths, not avoiding them.

PROMISING PRACTICE 2
Bite the Frog, Beat the Avoidance

You may have heard the phrase "eat the frog," a productivity mantra encouraging us to tackle our hardest or least pleasant task first. The idea is that addressing the toughest challenge head-on builds momentum. But what if the "frog" isn't just an unpleasant task, but an uncomfortable truth? Conflict avoidance often acts as an invisible force maintaining the status quo, rooted in our psychological drive to avoid discomfort and preserve harmony, even at the expense of justice and progress.

It shows up in our behaviors—deflecting tough conversations with humor, hesitating to give or receive feedback out of fear of distress, rushing to superficial agreement while silencing dissent. At an institutional level, it's masked by norms like overemphasizing politeness to stifle honest dialogue, clinging to tradition, or engaging in performative gestures that avoid deeper change. Recognizing these patterns is the first step in dismantling them.

(CONTINUED)

Steps to Recognize Conflict Avoidance in Yourself

1. **Notice discomfort:** Pay attention to moments where you feel uneasy about a conversation or task. Are you avoiding it to preserve comfort or avoid confrontation?

2. **Identify deflection habits:** Reflect on whether you change the topic, make jokes, or downplay serious issues to sidestep discomfort.

3. **Evaluate feedback patterns:** Consider whether fear of hurting feelings or being misunderstood stops you from giving (or receiving) honest feedback.

4. **Observe your reactions to criticism:** If feedback makes you defensive or dismissive, ask yourself why and what underlying fear might drive that response.

Steps to Recognize Conflict Avoidance in Systems

1. **Examine policies and traditions:** Look for rules or norms prioritizing "how we've always done it" over addressing systemic issues.

2. **Listen for silence:** Pay attention to who is not speaking up and whether dissent is discouraged or punished.

3. **Assess diversity efforts:** Consider whether initiatives address root inequities or focus only on symbolic gestures.

4. **Question the culture:** Observe whether politeness and professionalism are used to sideline critical conversations about inequity.

Face It, Fix It: Overcoming Conflict Avoidance

Once we understand the patterns of conflict avoidance to seek out, we can use that language and framing to overcome our own harmful behaviors:

Be curious, not judgmental.

When faced with discomfort, ask yourself: *Why am I feeling this way? What can I learn from this situation?* Shifting from a defensive mindset to one of curiosity can help you engage more constructively.

Discomfort is a growth spurt.

Growth often comes from resolving discomfort. Instead of retreating from challenging conversations, practice sitting with discomfort and listening deeply to others' perspectives.

Make room for real talk.

In institutions, leaders must create environments where employees feel safe to speak up without fear of retaliation. This includes actively seeking out and valuing dissenting voices.

Speak up, don't shut down.

Equip yourself and your organization with tools to navigate conflict constructively. This might include training in active listening, mediation, or nonviolent communication.

A Parting Note

I have intentionally chosen to exclude in-depth discussion of the transatlantic slave trade. This is not because it is irrelevant— it underpins so much of the systemic injustice we continue to face. Nerve is innate to Black people in this country. It is woven into our DNA, etched into our bones, and carried forward through generations.

Have you ever heard of epigenetics? It's the study of how the pain, stress, and struggle for survival that our ancestors experienced have altered the way our genes are expressed—meaning the trauma Black people have endured for centuries isn't just historical, it's biological, passed down through generations. The resilience and audacity required just to exist in a world committed to our demise are not learned behaviors but inherited necessities weighed against the very real threats of backlash, erasure, and violence. Our survival continues to demand that same inherited resilience.[25] But that's all I'll say for now. The subject deserves its own space, gravity, and reckoning. A space that feels like a family get-together for Sunday dinner. Again, if you know, you know . . .

3

Society's
Silent Partner

"Nice" is a contract signed in silence, subtly shaping our thoughts, feelings, and actions without us realizing it. Power dynamics, unspoken expectations, and the constant battle between authenticity and acceptance capture the universal challenge of navigating societal norms. Let's unpack how this contract binds us and why breaking it is so difficult.

The (Social) Proof Is in the Pudding

I adore Meryl Streep in *The Devil Wears Prada*. As Miranda Priestly, the imperious editor-in-chief of *Runway*, she reigns over a world of perfectionism and hierarchy. Her new assistant, Andy (played by Anne Hathaway), begins the job dismissive of the industry's values, considering herself a "serious" journalist taking a detour to pay the bills. But she soon finds herself drawn into *Runway*'s unspoken rules.

One memorable scene captures this shift. Andy snickers during a fashion spread meeting, finding the topic trivial. Miranda's sharp response—a breakdown of how Andy's blue sweater (pardon me, *cerulean* sweater) was influenced by the industry she mocks—unpacks the layers of influence shaping even Andy's disdain. It's a cutting reminder that no one is truly outside the system's reach. Fearing for her job, Andy turns to fashion editor Nigel (Stanley Tucci) for help. After a reluctant makeover, she returns to work in designer outfits, instantly noticing a shift in how colleagues perceive her—and even earning Miranda's approval. Seeking further acceptance, Andy dives deeper into the world she once ridiculed until it engulfs her.

It's a textbook example of *social proof*, the psychological phenomenon of looking to others to define what is acceptable or desirable. Humans are wired to emulate behaviors that bring approval or avoid conflict. In today's digital world, social proof plays out through curated social media feeds, where likes and shares subtly dictate what we value.

Niceness operates much the same way. This unspoken code of conduct pressures us to behave in ways that yield acceptance or avoid conflict—at the cost of authenticity.[1] Over time, this standard becomes unquestioned, much like Andy's acceptance of *Runway*'s culture. Recognizing these patterns allows us to disrupt them and make more intentional choices about how we engage with the world.

The Chemistry of Compliance

If social proof shows us how niceness subtly pressures individuals, frameworks in psychology and sociology reveal the mechanisms that sustain it. Niceness is a pervasive tool to regulate behavior, discourage conflict, and maintain societal cohesion.

To challenge its grip, we must unpack how these forces shape our interactions and decisions.

Psychology

In psychology—particularly social and behavioral psychology—the focus is often on how societal influences shape individual behavior and thought processes. Relevant concepts include:

- **Social norms:** The unwritten rules we internalize to gain acceptance or avoid disapproval, like invisible traffic signs guiding behavior. Just as Andy strives to fit in at *Runway*, many feel pressured to conform in school, the workplace, or our communities.

- **Behavioral conditioning:** Mechanisms like reinforcement and punishment (operant conditioning) that shape behavior and are influenced by societal expectations. This is similar to how you might use either treats or scolding to train your dog, so it learns what you want it to do or not to do; we learn what earns positive and negative responses from those around us.

- **Conformity and obedience:** Psychological processes that encourage individuals to align their behaviors with group norms or authority figures, as studied in classic experiments like Asch's conformity studies or Milgram's obedience studies. Picture a group of friends all agreeing on what movie to watch. Even if one person disagrees, they might go along with the group to avoid feeling left out.

- **Implicit bias:** Subconscious stereotypes shaped by cultural norms, like wearing tinted sunglasses that color your view without you realizing it. Just as Miranda dismisses

Andy for not "looking the part," biases about appearance, tone, and demeanor influence how we are judged and how we judge others.

Sociology

In sociology, the discussion commonly centers on social or institutional influence mechanisms—frameworks intended to maintain order and cohesion within a society. Relevant concepts include:

- **Social control:** Formal mechanisms (laws, regulations) and informal triggers (peer pressure, cultural norms) that enforce conformity to societal expectations. Think of a neighborhood watch program: laws set boundaries, but subtle signals, like a neighbor's disapproving look at an untidy yard, prompt compliance. At *Runway*, Andy's colleagues enforce cultural norms with side glances, snide comments, and exclusion—informal cues that, combined with Miranda's authority, pressure Andy to conform and maintain order.

- **Structural functionalism:** A perspective that views societal structures (like legal systems, education, or the media) as serving a purpose in maintaining stability, but also as systems of control. In a school system, for example, we teach students to raise their hand to speak. This introduces the concept that there is a particular order to how things must operate, conditioning them to follow rules without questioning them.

- **Conflict theory:** A framework that emphasizes how societal control reflects power dynamics. It often privileges dominant groups at the expense of marginalized groups. The stronger side makes the rules and benefits the most.

- **Symbolic interactionism:** Examines how social norms and roles are constructed through interaction, shaping behavior and identity. Consider the game Simon Says, where players are conditioned to follow the leader's instructions only if they are preceded by "Simon says." If they act without that cue, they are "out," reinforcing the importance of paying attention to social signals.

- **Hegemony:** Describes how dominant groups maintain control by shaping cultural norms and ideologies, making them appear natural and unquestionable (like a TV channel presenting only one perspective). Over time, this "echo chamber" discourages dissent and alternative ideas. Miranda's cerulean sweater monologue demonstrates hegemony, dismantling Andy's dismissal of fashion and revealing how even outsiders unknowingly conform to the system's influence.

The Undue Influence of Nice

In his classic book *Propaganda*, Edward Bernays explains that institutions depend on public acquiescence to maintain control. This compliance is achieved through undue influence—a mechanism that subtly shapes decisions using psychological and social pressures rather than overt coercion.

I recently watched *The Mind, Explained* on Netflix, where Dr. Nafees Hamid explores how sacred values—deeply held principles like freedom, loyalty, or environmental conservation—shape human behavior.[2] Sacred values aren't just beliefs; they're core to identity. Neuroscience shows that when these values are threatened, the brain's logic center (the dorsolateral prefrontal cortex) essentially shuts down, while emotional and social judgment areas activate. This explains why sacred values resist compromise, even in the face of reason or evidence.

Consider free speech. For many, it's a sacred value, so even suggesting limits—like banning hate speech—triggers emotional resistance. It's not about agreeing with harmful language, but about protecting a principle seen as inviolable. Similarly, environmental conservation is sacred to others. Proposals for limited deforestation to boost economic growth often face passionate opposition because the cause transcends practicality and is deeply tied to identity and morality.

Dr. Hamid's research highlights how social exclusion can deepen radicalization, especially when sacred values are involved. His team found that some young men already committed to extremist ideologies processed their sacred values—like religious devotion—without deliberation, making them more willing to defend those values through violence.[3] The broader research suggests that in contexts of alienation or disconnection, even non-sacred concerns—such as local grievances or political ideologies—can take on sacred weight, transforming personal discontent into causes worth fighting or dying for.[4]

So what's the link to niceness? Like sacred values, niceness operates quietly, shaping our behavior in profound ways. It becomes an unspoken expectation: Stay agreeable, avoid confrontation, and maintain harmony. This compliance reinforces social norms and discourages critical thinking or dissent.

While niceness may not appear harmful, its subtle influence is far-reaching. Like sacred values, it resists scrutiny because it feels embedded in what's "right" or "normal." The threat of exclusion further reinforces this dynamic. Nobody wants to "ruin the vibe" or risk alienation by speaking up. Over time, niceness traps people in passive acceptance, stifling authenticity and accountability.

Recognizing this parallel allows us to reframe niceness not as benign social glue but as a tool of undue influence. Breaking the silent contract requires understanding how niceness operates as both a psychological shield and a societal mechanism for maintaining the existing order.

The Need for Belonging

At its core, the drive to be nice stems from a fundamental human need for belonging. Psychologist Abraham Maslow's hierarchy of needs highlights social connection as critical for psychological health.[5] To feel accepted, people often suppress their true feelings and desires, aligning with group norms.[6] Like Andy in *The Devil Wears Prada*, many choose conformity over self-expression to avoid exclusion, often without realizing the cost.

This tension between conformity and authenticity can lead to moral injury—psychological distress caused when actions, or inaction, violate deeply held values. While initially associated with soldiers, moral injury manifests in everyday contexts when people stay silent in the face of injustice to protect their social standing. This silence erodes self-worth and integrity, turning niceness from a survival strategy into a source of harm, perpetuating a system prioritizing keeping the peace over doing what is right.

"It's Not a Lie if You Believe It"

Fans of *Seinfeld* will recognize George Costanza's advice—"It's not a lie if you believe it"—as the ultimate justification for self-deception, offered to Jerry as he prepared for a polygraph test. It's the same mindset Andy adopts in *The Devil Wears Prada* when she convinces herself that adapting to *Runway*'s world is temporary. While things didn't work out for Jerry or Andy, Leon Festinger's theory of cognitive dissonance explains the underlying psychological force: When our actions clash with our view of ourselves as good, fair, or authentic, we justify them to maintain internal consistency.[7] Whether it's Jerry trying to beat a polygraph or Andy rationalizing her complicity at *Runway*, this self-deception keeps people stuck, choosing niceness and conformity over the discomfort of confronting harmful systems.

Institutional Manipulation

In their landmark study of media manipulation and propaganda in democratic societies, *Manufacturing Consent*, Noam Chomsky and Edward S. Herman argue that media, politics, and education shape public opinion to preserve the status quo. By elevating niceness as a virtue, institutions condition individuals to see dissent as harmful—what Chomsky and Herman call "manufactured consent." Schools teach "respect for authority," casting questions about injustice as insubordination, while governments label activists and whistleblowers as "un-American" or "radical."

This gaslighting erodes confidence in personal judgment, discouraging challenges to authority and sustaining harmful systems—especially in the workplace. Corporate culture rewards being "team-oriented" and "positive" while branding critiques of inequity or toxicity as unprofessional. At *Runway*, employees often suppressed their instincts to avoid running afoul of Miranda or being labeled "difficult" or "negative."

In *The Managed Heart*, sociologist Arlie Hochschild exposes how emotional labor (the regulation or suppression of one's feelings to meet societal expectations) disproportionately burdens women along with Black, Indigenous, and Latinx people and other marginalized groups, who must suppress authentic emotions not just to keep their jobs but to avoid harmful stereotypes. This expectation enables corporations to extract both productivity and psychological compliance from their employees, silencing calls for fair treatment, better conditions, and systemic change.

The result? A workforce—and society—disarmed of its ability to challenge oppression, trapped in a cycle of conformity masquerading as virtue, focusing on conflict avoidance at the expense of progress.

Consider the tobacco industry: fully aware that smoking caused cancer, it funded biased research, sowed doubt about scientific consensus, and launched massive ad campaigns to gaslight the public. Similarly, Purdue Pharma marketed Oxy-Contin as a non-addictive painkiller while training representatives to dismiss addiction concerns as "pseudo-addiction," fueling the opioid crisis and devastating millions of families; and Pacific Gas and Electric lied to the residents of Hinkley, California, about poisoning the local water supply with chromium (a story made famous by the 2000 film *Erin Brockovich*, with Julia Roberts in the starring role). These are just a few examples of how corporations manipulate public trust to cover up harm.

Much like how the fictional *Runway* magazine's polished facade hid a world of ruthless hierarchy, institutions rely on niceness to mask exploitation, ensuring the system thrives even as it harms. Unmasking this manipulation is the first step toward progress.

PROMISING PRACTICE 3
Ask Questions That Slay

Did you know there is an art and science to how we ask questions?[8] Accepting surface-level answers or assuming that existing perspectives are complete is not enough. To uncover root causes, include marginalized voices, and foster deeper understanding, we must intentionally ask

(CONTINUED)

questions that challenge assumptions and broaden the scope of inquiry. However, asking the right questions is only part of the equation. Inquiry and advocacy determine the quality and impact of our conversations, driving collaboration and better decision-making:

- **Advocacy** is the act of clearly and persuasively advancing your views. It involves explaining your perspective, presenting evidence, and advocating for your conclusions.

- **Inquiry** is the act of exploring others' viewpoints to deepen mutual understanding. Effective inquiry involves asking thoughtful, open-ended questions, listening deeply, and seeking to understand and challenge one's assumptions.

Balancing these two modes of communication creates what strategy expert Roger Martin calls *assertive inquiry*, a process that combines clear advocacy with genuine curiosity.[9] An overemphasis on advocacy can lead to entrenchment, as too much focus on "winning" an argument may shut down varying perspectives and foster resistance. Relying solely on inquiry, however, can undermine your expertise and may prevent actionable conclusions. Effectively utilizing both allows leaders and teams to foster a shared understanding that leads to better outcomes. Think again of Miranda Priestly's cerulean sweater monologue—she doesn't just defend the significance of fashion; she reframes Andy's dismissal of it with a mix of assertion and explanation. What if Andy had met Miranda's advocacy with curiosity rather than defensiveness? The result could have been a valid exchange, not just a master class in mic dropping.

The 4WH Framework

Asking *Who*, *What*, *When*, *Where*, and *How* provides a structured approach to uncovering varying perspectives and ensuring inclusive solutions:

- **Who** questions help identify stakeholders, power dynamics, and gaps in representation, ensuring a more inclusive and equitable approach.

- **What** questions emphasize clarity and accountability, helping uncover overlooked details and blind spots.

- **When** questions help establish timing, which is critical in understanding the urgency of an issue and avoiding unnecessary delays that perpetuate harm.

- **Where** questions focus on actionable areas and encourage a targeted approach to change.

- **How** questions translate insights into action, driving the practical implementation of solutions.

Why Not Ask "Why?"

The 4WH questions provide concrete details that help us garner understanding. Asking *Why* elicits subjective interpretations of causation or motivation.[10] For example, instead of asking, "Why didn't you speak up in that meeting?" you might ask: "What factors made you hesitant to speak up? Who was in the room, and how did their presence influence you? Where have similar situations occurred? How would the outcome have changed if you had spoken up?" These questions provide a stronger foundation for understanding and help uncover systemic dynamics and behavioral patterns.

PROMISING PRACTICE 4
Don't Let Assumptions Run the Show

Organizational theorist Chris Argyris introduced the Ladder of Inference to explain how we leap from observing reality to making decisions, often guided by unconscious biases and assumptions.[11] And yes, as the joke goes, "When you assume, you make an ass out of you and me!" This tool helps us unpack the societal and psychological influences shaping our choices, offering a way to make smarter, bias-aware decisions. Let's see how the ladder works as a lens for critical thinking:

Ground level: Observe reality

Notice observable data and facts.

Ask yourself: What am I seeing, hearing, or experiencing? What objective evidence is available?

Example: In a workplace meeting, you notice that one person speaks significantly less than others.

First rung: Select data

Focus on specific details while ignoring others.

Ask yourself: Am I selectively noticing details based on biases? What might I be missing?

Example: You might interpret the quiet person as disengaged but not have considered other factors, like the meeting format or power dynamics.

Second rung: Interpret data

Assign meaning to the selected data.

Ask yourself: What meaning am I assigning to this data, and why? Is this interpretation the only possibility?

Example: You assume the person's silence means they lack valuable input, but what other possible explanations might there be?

Third rung: Form assumptions

Add interpretation to what's happening.

Ask yourself: What assumptions am I making, and how might they reflect my biases?

Example: You assume the person's silence indicates disengagement rather than being a reflection of the environment or their communication style.

Top rung: Take action

Make decisions based on your assumptions, shaping outcomes.

Ask yourself: What actions am I taking based on these assumptions? Are they equitable and informed?

Example: You might exclude the quiet person from future conversations, reinforcing inequities in decision-making and group dynamics.

At every step, pause to reflect on how observations, interpretations, and assumptions might limit your perspective.

Unpacking the Cost of Niceness

The roots of niceness run deep in the American psyche, a survival strategy crafted within an oppressive system that demands conformity over integrity. It binds our sense of worth to compliance, our moral virtue to harmony, and our survival to silence. But the cost is far too high.

I feel this cost acutely, not just as a scholar and practitioner, but as a mother raising a Black daughter in a world that equates gentleness with weakness and authenticity with risk. I've seen my smile weaponized, my silence extracted—not as a sign of peace, but as a means of preservation. If people understood the jagged edges I've swallowed to keep the waters calm, perhaps they would stop demanding this brand of "nice."

I hope my daughter never has to make impossible choices—between her authenticity and her safety, between her brilliance and the comfort of others. I hope she never learns the painful calculus of shrinking herself to avoid being labeled difficult, aggressive, or unkind.

Much like Andy's realization in *The Devil Wears Prada*, where she questions whether the world she's conformed to aligns with her values, we must confront the silent contracts we sign and the price they exact.

I know this is a lot to take in. This is the "Think" section, after all. Understanding *how* and *why* niceness quietly shapes our lives is vital before we can break free from its grip. Now that we've laid the groundwork, let's step into a world of possibility together. It's time to move forward—boldly, authentically, and with the power to create real change.

PART II
FEEL

4

Flow or Crash

Part I gave us the foundations—mental models, history, and frameworks. Those concepts are all largely unchanging. No matter how hard the book banners try, the events that shaped our past aren't going anywhere. "It is what it is," as the kids say. Part II explores how we experience, process, and respond to the world around us. This section is about utilizing our emotional intelligence to adapt and move forward. This chapter will help you understand where you are in that journey.

Be Like Water

When I was a kid, everybody was kung-fu fighting. Everyone wanted to fight like Bruce Lee, Chuck Norris, or, in my house, Leroy Green. We perfected our "crane technique," just like Mr. Miyagi taught Daniel-san. We all had our favorite Ninja Turtle or Power Ranger, and video games like *Street Fighter* and *Mortal Kombat* were all the rage. And we daydreamed about what it would be like to go on adventures like Rocky, Colt, and Tum-Tum in the *3 Ninjas* movie.

"Now, water can flow or it can crash. Be water, my friend." This famous quote from Bruce Lee reflects his martial arts philosophy: letting go of rigid beliefs and being open-minded and flexible to adjust to the situation.[1] Just like water adapts to its surroundings, so must we—the question isn't whether we should adapt, but how we do it. Armed with an understanding of "nice" as a construct, our response can be to go with the flow or to meet that temptation head-on. To "crash." Otherwise, we risk simply being carried away by the current of niceness that pervades our society.

My dad passed away in 2022. A minister and IT guru, he was also a third degree Taekwondo black belt and part-time instructor. My brothers tagged along to his lessons, and he was the undisputed sensei in our living room dojo, where we play-fought and practiced moves we saw on TV. He was never a violent man, but he understood a crucial truth: Niceness doesn't protect you from harm.

Growing up as one of the few Black families on a tiny island—Guam, USA—my siblings and I learned early on that the world didn't always meet us with kindness or fairness. We endured relentless bullying on the school bus, in the classroom, and in our neighborhood. The taunts and slurs were constant reminders of how we were seen. Being a churchgoing family, we were inundated with the typical advice to "turn the other cheek" or "kill them with kindness." But the bullies who tormented us didn't care how "nice" we were; they thrived on cruelty, on making us feel small.

One day, my dad sat us all down and said something that none of us expected to hear. He promised we would never be in trouble with him for defending ourselves. He didn't want us to go looking for a fight, but he assured us that protecting ourselves was more critical than being "good" or "nice"—especially when our only "crime" was existing while Black. We were allowed to fight back.

My older brother probably had it worse than the rest of us (I'm the second-oldest of eight siblings; did I mention that?). In his fifth-grade class, there was one kid who decided it was his mission to make my brother's life miserable. He and his friends threw spit wads, tripped him in the hallways, stole his lunch, and hurled racial slurs.

But one day, he finally pushed too far. My brother, fed up, delivered a roundhouse kick to the bully's face. The word around school was that you could see my brother's chalk-dusted foot imprinted on that boy's cheek. The teacher, who had seen the bullying play out over time, backed my brother up with the principal. That kid deserved it, to be frank, and the teacher knew it. And my dad was true to his word. He even took my brother out for ice cream.

(Can I just say one thing right here? In all of these situations, there were adults present. Adults with authority and opportunity. Adults who witnessed the bullying, the racism, the cruelty. And did nothing. We were just kids! Imagine if those adults had had the nerve to intervene before violence became our only option. Imagine if their authority had been used to protect us, not just to mete out punishment when things went too far. Their inaction spoke volumes. Their unwillingness to disrupt the status quo left us to fend for ourselves. Their belated support did little other than to placate, and came too late to erase the hurt. And so, the burden fell to us. Systems of power operate similarly ... yet I digress.)

As it happens, that boy's family lived not far from us—on Guam, no one really lives too far from anyone else! Not long after the incident in the classroom, just as my family arrived home from the store, we saw him walking through the neighborhood with his father. As we unloaded our groceries from the car, that kid took it upon himself to start shouting at my brother. I can't tell you everything he said, something about a cheap shot, but he definitely decided to throw in a couple of "n" words for good measure. I was shocked, not by what he said, which was nothing new, but that he said it right in front of our parents—and his!

I *can* tell you that I'll never forget what happened next. My brother was ready for round two. Even my mother, ever the peacemaker, was beside herself. My dad, calm and measured as always, said nothing, but simply held up his hand, quieting us all immediately. We watched as he walked over to the boy and his father, smirking next to him, and said something in a tone too low for us to hear. I could see his face—the tightness in his jaw, the way his nostrils flared. I knew that look. My dad was angry. Whatever he said that day, I think we can assume it wasn't "nice." Then he walked back to the car, picked up some bags, and headed inside.

Something immediately shifted. I could never get my dad to reveal what he'd said, but whatever it was, that boy apparently passed the word on to his friends. From that moment on, they never bothered us again. Whenever he saw us around the neighborhood, the boy who'd once taken pride in his cruelty would just sheepishly nod in our direction. And he always called my dad "sir." I couldn't help but sneer a little.

That moment taught me a powerful lesson: Niceness didn't change that boy's behavior; nerve did. Nice is passive. It waits for the right moment, system, or ally. Nerve, on the other hand, insists on action. It doesn't wait for permission. It doesn't rely on others to do the right thing. My dad didn't sugarcoat the situation or try to make the boy feel comfortable about his actions. He leaned into the discomfort, demanded accountability, and set a standard for how we deserved to be treated. And his willingness to take action changed everything.

Four Characteristics of Nice That Hinder Progress

In a world where too many people are content to stand by, hoping things will sort themselves out, there is a void for someone to come along with the nerve to say, "Enough is enough." But if we're going to change the world, we'll need to start by examining ourselves. Our relationship with nice has conditioned us into submission, involuntarily aligning ourselves with systems that diminish individual and collective agency. In fact, many behaviors that keep us stuck in a cycle of submission often go unnoticed. Recognizing them is the first step toward breaking free and creating change. Conditioned constraints we must overcome include:

- **Lack of awareness:** A cognitive gap that prevents recognizing how niceness perpetuates systemic inequities. This includes ignoring historical context, minimizing the role of power dynamics, and failing to examine assumptions and biases critically.

- **Lack of accountability:** An emotional resistance to discomfort that prevents engaging fully with challenges, critique, or brutal truths. This fragility often manifests as defensiveness, withdrawal, or avoidance when confronted with inequities or the harm caused by niceness.

- **Lack of agency:** A failure to take action that challenges power dynamics or creates systemic change, often due to fear of disrupting the current order or being seen as "too assertive." This disempowers individuals and communities, reinforcing hierarchies.

- **Lack of adaptability:** A resistance to growth and change, treating failures or setbacks as end points instead of opportunities. This limits progress by avoiding critical reflection on past actions or strategies.

We must question how and why systems work as they do, embrace hard truths, and take responsibility. Rather than avoiding discomfort, use it to grow. Challenge injustice, speak up, support others, and take even small steps toward change. Reflect on what works and what doesn't, and refine your approach to sustain meaningful impact.

Over the years, I've gathered insights from communications, DEI, sociology, psychology, activism, and community building, blending science and art. People often ask, *"How do you do it? How do you show up like this?"* For a long time, I insisted there was no formula, no road map. But while there is no quick fix, reflection and experience have shown me that my approach does follow a framework.

This book brings together years of research and personal experience, combining them into a tool kit for moving through the world as a trustworthy change agent. It's how I've learned to navigate systems and challenge norms. This isn't just theory. Born of trial and error and forged in the crucible of discomfort, these ideas have been refined through years of living my sacred values out loud.

The tools are a set of simple, introspective observations on behaviors, thought patterns, and comfort zones to help you locate yourself on what I call the *Nice to Nerve Continuum* (Table 1). Once you identify your starting point, you can apply the Promising Practices I outline. These tactics aren't one-size-fits-all—they allow for incremental or radical change, depending on your readiness, capacity, and audacity (ha!). Review the following chart, assess each stage, and reflect on which statements best align with your mindset and actions.

Table 1: The Nice to Nerve Continuum

KEY ELEMENTS	→ NICE TO NERVE CONTINUUM →				
	Nice	**Neutral**	**Nudge**	**Navigate**	**Nerve**
Characteristics	Prioritizes politeness, avoids conflict, and maintains superficial harmony	Remains impartial, avoids clear positions, and sidesteps contentious issues	Encourages incremental steps rather than addressing profound or systemic issues directly	Actively navigates discomfort to address root causes and guide others toward meaningful action	Boldly disrupts harmful systems, prioritizing justice and transformation over comfort to drive lasting change
Goal	To appear agreeable and pleasant, often prioritizing comfort over truth or justice	To avoid taking sides or rocking the boat, often under the guise of objectivity	To foster minor progress and test the waters for more significant conversations	To create meaningful, sustained progress by addressing systemic barriers while fostering collaboration	To advance equity and justice through courageous, transformative action
Pitfalls	Masks deeper problems, enabling harm and suppressing critical conversations	Through failure to act, perpetuates inequities and signals that issues aren't worth addressing	Lacks boldness, risking tokenism and performative gestures without deeper change	Requires significant effort and risks burnout without adequate support	Invites backlash and discomfort, creating potential for conflict or alienation
Example	Saying, "Let's agree to disagree" without addressing systemic inequities	Saying, "I don't see color," which dismisses the lived experiences of marginalized groups	Saying, "Let's start with a training" instead of addressing structural inequities	Saying, "This will take time, but we need to overhaul our policies to ensure equity"	Saying, "Our leadership lacks representation, and we need to restructure immediately to fix it"

Where you are on this continuum today should be viewed not as a final destination but a launching pad. Consider which behaviors from the next stage you'd like to adopt. Then, prepare to step into vulnerability, embrace discomfort, and, ultimately, summon the nerve to demand change.

This journey requires resilience, reflection, and relentless commitment. It will challenge you with hard questions and uncomfortable truths. It's about honesty in where you stand, boldness in where you're headed, and an uncompromising pursuit of justice—not just for yourself, but for the world you want to create. And let's be clear: It *should* feel uncomfortable. Unpacking conditioning and unlearning decades of gaslighting is no small task.

Remember, there's no finish line. Moving from nice to nerve is an ongoing evolution, shifting as you go. But if you commit to the work, you'll realize the journey *is* the transformation. It's not about reaching an end point—it's about *Becoming* (shout out to Michelle Obama!).

Outwit, Outplay, Outlast

Some will recognize that heading from the reality show *Survivor*. Like the show, real life demands adaptability to navigate mental and physical challenges. As a behavioral communications consultant, I use a *to/from* framework to map shifts from current to desired behaviors, offering clear direction and action steps. But this isn't just a professional tool—as a Black woman, it's deeply personal.

In a society that has long prized conformity and discouraged dissent, authenticity has often invited punishment. Forced to conceal our culture, physical attributes, emotions, and language, marginalized people have developed various psychological strategies, such as *tuning, covering, masking,* and *code switching,* as survival mechanisms.

Tuning refers to adjusting one's behavior to align with dominant cultural norms to avoid rejection or violence. During the postcolonial and industrial eras, the American ideal of the "melting pot" sought to erase cultural differences in favor of a singular national identity. Immigrants, Indigenous peoples, and enslaved Africans were pressured to suppress their languages, traditions, and beliefs to gain acceptance.

Covering became a common survival strategy during the Civil Rights Movement and beyond, as Black Americans and other marginalized groups downplayed aspects of their identities to navigate workplaces and public spaces dominated by White norms. I've experienced this firsthand: Early in my career, a colleague commented on my natural curls, suggesting they were "for the weekend." The next day—and for over a decade—I straightened my hair, not out of preference, but to meet unspoken expectations of professionalism and avoid further scrutiny.

Masking has deep roots in American history, from slavery to Jim Crow to today's corporate America, where Black individuals have learned to conceal genuine emotions, hiding fear, anger, or frustration behind a mask of deference. I've certainly smiled and nodded my way through plenty of meetings. One misstep could mean being labeled "hostile," "difficult," or "not a team player," leading to poor reviews, stalled advancement, or worse.

Have you ever met a coworker socially and noticed they seemed like a different person? This isn't a case of split personalities, but likely the result of code switching. Black Americans, immigrants, and other historically marginalized groups have long had to alternate between authentic cultural expressions and behaviors deemed "acceptable" by mainstream society. It's not about denying who we are, but navigating the unwritten rules of two distinct cultural realities.

These adaptations are rooted in a history of systemic oppression. Over generations, they have become ingrained habits. The flawed ideal of "colorblindness" is a product of this legacy, promoting the idea that seeing everyone as the same will dispel racism. While seemingly well-intentioned, it erases individual histories and lived experiences, weakening us by valuing conformity over the strength of diversity.

Recognizing and managing these emotional dynamics is critical. Emotional awareness and intelligence help us identify when we're dissociating from our true selves to meet external expectations. The ability to plot, monitor, and adapt behaviors becomes an unspoken strategy—a necessity to navigate spaces where we must carefully manage perceptions. By understanding how and why we feel a certain way, we can bridge that gap, aligning our responses with our authentic selves. This practice not only fosters personal growth but also challenges the systems that demand disconnection.

Table 2 reflects lived experiences described across the continuum. The list is not exhaustive, but represents behavioral patterns I have most commonly encountered as a communications and DEI practitioner. Do any of these feel familiar to you? By naming and understanding these patterns, you can disrupt ingrained behaviors and boldly move toward lasting transformation.

Table 2: From Nice to Nerve Behavioral Framework

NICE	NERVE
Inauthentic self (conformity)	Chosen self
Avoiding conflict at all costs	Addressing conflict with courage
Seeking external validation	Grounded in self-worth

Flow or Crash

NICE	NERVE
Over-apologizing for asserting needs or boundaries	Apologizing only when necessary
Suppressing personal needs	Expressing personal needs
Fear of disappointing others	Setting and honoring boundaries
People-pleasing	Prioritizing mutual respect
Withholding honest feedback	Offering constructive feedback
Over-focusing on being liked	Focusing on being respected
Indirect and avoidant asks	Direct and clear communication
Agreeing to avoid discomfort	Disagreeing with integrity
Overextending to avoid rejection	Saying "no" when needed
Hiding emotions to "keep the peace"	Expressing emotions authentically
Conforming to fit in	Celebrating individuality
Deflecting compliments	Accepting compliments graciously
Avoiding difficult conversations	Initiating meaningful dialogue
Allowing fear to dictate actions	Taking action despite fear
Over-apologizing for opinions	Owning and standing by opinions
Using vague language to avoid offending	Speaking with clarity and intention
Overusing "softeners" like *just, sorry,* or *maybe*	Communicating directly and confidently
Agreeing verbally while disagreeing internally	Voicing honest disagreements respectfully
Avoiding tough conversations to "keep the peace"	Initiating necessary, solution-focused discussions
Offering insincere praise to prevent discomfort	Providing meaningful, constructive feedback
Using filler words and phrases like "I'm not the expert but . . .," "Does that make sense?" or "Can I say something real quick?" to downplay opinions	Stating opinions assertively and concisely
Nodding or smiling to mask disagreement	Using body language that matches true intent

A Note on Neutrality

I don't believe true neutrality is achievable. It's included in the continuum because many people strive for it or claim it's possible, so I've accounted for it reluctantly. Arguments for neutrality fracture when we consider power dynamics, personal values, or human subjectivity. For example, imagine a teacher trying to stay "neutral" during a class discussion about racism. If the teacher avoids addressing the topic to avoid taking a stance, their silence could be seen as accepting this injustice, which might make students from marginalized groups feel unsupported. Our decisions—what to say and what to leave out—are shaped by our experiences and biases, even if we don't realize it.

Since neutrality often serves the status quo, we must be intentional about how we engage, aiming for objectivity by recognizing our biases and trying to mitigate their impact on others. But not all action is good—history shows us that nerve can be weaponized, too.

When Nerve Is Used to Harm

A caveat on building your nerve: It can drive positive change, but also harm. Disruption for its own sake helps no one (again, no one likes an asshole). Worse, history is full of bad actors who've weaponized behavior change, using communication to sow division, consolidate power, and dehumanize others.

These individuals and movements did not concern themselves with restraint. They certainly had nerve—but they used that fortitude to act in ways that oppressed the vulnerable.

The most infamous example has to be Nazi Germany under Adolf Hitler and his minister of propaganda, Joseph Goebbels. The Nazi regime expertly wielded communication to spread anti-Semitic hatred, promote Aryan supremacy, and justify unspeakable atrocities. Through films, posters, speeches, and newspapers, they positioned Jews, Romani people, LGBTQIA+ individuals, and other marginalized groups as subhuman threats to German society. The results were devastating: a cultural and psychological framework that exploited fear, manufactured hatred, and allowed ordinary citizens to justify participation in genocide, tolerating the horrors of the Holocaust.

Closer to home, former Confederate leaders and sympathizers developed the "Lost Cause" narrative to reframe the South's defeat in the Civil War as a noble, honorable struggle. This communication strategy sought to whitewash the actual cause of the war—the preservation of slavery—and replace it with a myth about states' rights, Southern honor, and the supposed benevolence of enslavers. Through textbooks, statues, speeches, and commemorative events, the Lost Cause narrative painted the Confederacy as a gallant underdog and minimized the horrors of slavery. This wasn't just about rewriting history; it was about sustaining White supremacy. It justified Jim Crow laws, racial segregation, and the disenfranchisement of Black Americans for generations.

Nerve to Build, Not Destroy

We need to recognize this reality and respond wisely. Nerve isn't inherently virtuous—when wielded with malice, it causes harm. Our task isn't just to have nerve, but to use it for the right reasons, and to act with courage and integrity even when retaliation feels tempting. The best revenge is not becoming the person who harmed you.

That doesn't mean resorting to passive niceness. As Toni Morrison urged, we must have the nerve not just to do things differently, but to *do a different thing*.[2] This means rejecting harm and oppression, and using communication and action to build a world of equity, justice, and inclusion. True disruption challenges harmful systems without continuing the cycle of harm.

In a world where bad actors sow harm, our strongest response is to match their resolve with our own, creating a world where harm cannot thrive. The nerve to oppress is real, evident in policies, slogans, and movements that impede or roll back progress. But we have a choice. Having nerve isn't just about standing up to bullies—it's about standing up for something better.

PROMISING PRACTICE 5
How's Your Spirit?

Sometimes, along the journey, the best way to grow is to stop and check in with yourself. Asking *"How's your spirit today?"* helps determine how you're feeling and whether you're staying true to what matters to you. Three key needs shape your choices:

- **Autonomy:** Are you making choices that match your values?

- **Competence:** Do you feel confident and capable in what you're doing?

- **Relatedness:** Are you connecting with others in meaningful ways?[3]

Reflecting on these questions can help you better understand what drives you, what holds you back, and how to be braver and kinder to yourself and others.

Ask yourself:

- Have you ever wanted to stand up to someone but didn't know how? What held you back?

- Have you ever felt invisible to those with the power to help? How did that shape your view of fairness and justice?

- How would you feel if someone told you it's okay to break the rules and stand up for yourself—empowered or unsure? Why?

- Have you ever reached a breaking point where taking action felt risky but necessary? What gave you courage in that moment?

- In moments of conflict, what emotions arise? Would you demand action, like my mom, or stay calm but firm, like my dad? What does your response reveal about how conflict has shaped you?

- If you had to confront someone who caused harm, would you prioritize their comfort or embrace discomfort to make it clear the harm was unacceptable?

- How do you define the difference between being nice and being courageous? Can you recall a time when you chose comfort over truth—when you were "nice" instead of courageous? How might the outcome have changed if you'd had the nerve to confront the harm?

Self-reflection and self-care are vital. Asking *"How's your spirit today?"* creates space to pause, recognize what strengthens you or holds you back, and embrace courage. It's about progress, not perfection. Checking in with your spirit shifts you from "being nice" to standing up for what's right—while staying true to who you are.

5

Start a
Burn Book!

J ust in case you didn't read that title carefully, it's *start a burn book*, not *start burning a book*. Again, just in case. Words matter. Didn't you see the movie *Mean Girls*? Anyone? Of course you did, so you'll understand the reference. But anyway...

In 2013, my then-employer brought in a consultant as we developed the next iteration of our five-year strategic plan. Her process included an unconventional exercise: keeping a weekly creative journal. The goal? To help us shift our perspectives on the problems we were solving and uncover new ways of thinking. It wasn't for jotting down mean thoughts about our coworkers (and definitely not about people who, in the words of *Mean Girls*, "don't even go here!"). So, not a "burn book" exactly, but it was more fun to think of it that way.

I vividly recall the visceral reaction my colleagues and I had when she introduced the idea. There were audible groans, and grimaces were exchanged at the thought of keeping a work diary. The skepticism in the room was palpable, but we obliged—because, after all, *the consultant is always right!* Writing down our observations and reflections felt unfamiliar, even uncomfortable at first. But as the weeks went on, the impact became undeniable. Capturing our thoughts on paper allowed us to begin seeing patterns, questioning assumptions, and approaching challenges with fresh eyes.

What initially felt like unwelcome homework became one of the most valuable tools I've encountered. It was more than just documenting thoughts—it became an intentional process of uncovering the hidden messages and practices we'd unquestioningly accepted. Journaling daily allowed me to spotlight "rules" I'd internalized and unspoken norms I'd never questioned. Our burn books were not about pettiness or gossip, but about burning the assumptions that held us back. I was so struck by the clarity and growth the practice afforded that I've kept a work journal ever since—it has become a cornerstone of how I process ideas, emotions, and experiences.

As it turns out, journaling is a science-backed tool. Studies show that it helps regulate our emotional responses to external stimuli, reducing stress, fostering resilience, and enhancing cognitive processing.[1] It also enables our brains to make sense of complex experiences by translating abstract thoughts into tangible words. This process creates clarity, strengthens problem-solving skills, and builds the mental agility to navigate personal and professional challenges.

Think of it this way: Creating your own burn book doesn't just expose what's holding you back—it provides you with a tool to move forward.

*(As you progress through these chapters, and along the continuum from nice to nerve, it is critically important to realize that **these shifts are within your control**. You can't change history or the psychological frameworks that brought us all here, but you can alter your perspectives, reactions, and behaviors.)*

How Our Brains Make Sense of Experiences

It's a myth that we use only 10 percent of our brains. In reality, we use 100 percent, even if we're unaware of how or when those parts work.[2] This truth about our brains' capacity reflects how we approach—or resist—change. Like our brains, the organizations we are part of (workplaces, schools, places of worship—any space where power is structured) are complex systems shaped by habits, environments, and assumptions. We grow so comfortable with the familiar that we fail to notice when those routines no longer serve us.

In neurology, *conscious perception* is when your brain recognizes and makes sense of what you're experiencing—a sound, a sight, or a feeling. It's the brain "switching on the light bulb" and connecting the dots. When you hear a noise, your brain processes it and connects it to a specific identity: a dog barking, a car horn, or your favorite late-'90s pop ballad. It's how we turn sensory information into meaningful experiences. It also works by triggering a response. For example, when you hear a phone ring, your brain is conditioned to respond by answering it (or at least checking the caller ID to decide whether or not to send suspected spammers or any family-members-who-you-still-love-but-just-can't-even-with-them-right-now to voicemail).

When it comes to our organizations, conscious perception allows us to recognize what's happening beneath the surface. We must train ourselves to see past the familiar ways of operating and identify the systems that have outlived their usefulness. This shift is crucial for changemakers because you can't fix a problem until you recognize it's there. One of my very favorite humans is James Baldwin, who aptly pointed out, "Not everything that is faced can be changed, but nothing can be changed until it is faced."[3] Having said that, once you recognize the hidden cultural gaps, you have to act. Refusal to do so is how organizations get mired in problematic processes and routines and become stagnant.

This is where the power of perspective comes into play. Do you remember those Magic Eye posters that were popular in the '90s? You know, the ones where if you went kind of cross-eyed and stared at them long enough, an image of dolphins or something would appear out of the shapes and colors? Optical illusions like these can vividly demonstrate how our brains process the world around us. They show us how we overlook what's right before us, seeing only what we've been conditioned to see. But the moment something shifts—when you finally spot the hidden image—you can never unsee it. That shift is transformative.

Organizations operate in much the same way. We can become so accustomed to the current state of affairs that we stop questioning it. We don't recognize the outdated processes or unchallenged biases that keep us from progressing. But once our perspective shifts—once we see the inefficiencies, inequities, or possibilities we missed before—we can't go back. The change is permanent, and so is the growth potential.

Another example of how perspective shifts work is the famous "My Wife and My Mother-in-Law" image.[4] I'm sure you've probably come across this at some point. Depending on what the mind focuses on, some people see an older woman looking off to the left, while others see a young woman facing away. Two realities exist at once, but it takes an active shift in perception to see both. (Hello, nuance!) The lived experience that a person brings to a given situation influences what image they are able to see. By taking the time to engage and possessing a willingness to be open to new worldviews, we can see things in ways that may not have been readily apparent to us. (Hello, empathy!)

Similarly, detrimental cultural practices in many organizations are illusions that can go unnoticed simply because we're used to them or have been conditioned to accept them as the norm. We see only one version of reality. When we consciously shift our perspective, a new, previously hidden reality emerges, and we can recognize the underlying messages or problems. But once aware, we are forced to reckon with a newfound responsibility—it is up to us to push for change.

Shift Happens

Asking questions, challenging outdated methods, and suggesting new ideas through conversation unlocks potential. It also invites others to be part of the solution, sparking conversations that drive group alignment and collective action.[5]

Just like a map helps you see where you are and where you want to go, journaling helps track shifts in your thinking. It reveals what you've accepted as "just the way things are" and challenges you to see new possibilities. By revealing the hidden gaps between what people say and what they truly experience, we can uncover deeper truths often masked by niceness.

Imagine a corporation that invites raw feedback—a place where employees are encouraged to voice what they feel but rarely say aloud, addressing the gaps that leave others feeling unheard and unappreciated. Then, take it a step further. Apply that to each stage of the employee experience, charting how employees are welcomed, trained, and supported, and where they feel lost. This will allow you to identify barriers and sticking points, like a policy that unintentionally excludes some people, opening up opportunities for improvement that might have otherwise passed you by.

Incorporating empathy into our processes enables us to address real needs and foster meaningful change. Conversations like these allow us to see the world through someone else's eyes, to walk the proverbial mile in their shoes. In any given workplace, executives make decisions, but frontline employees feel the impact most. Have you ever seen the TV show *Undercover Boss*? Engendering transparency in our organizations helps us to see the hidden struggles, challenge outdated norms, and create bolder, more authentic solutions.

Sometimes the best ideas come from the people furthest from the norm. By accounting for the experiences of the outliers—those who don't fit neatly into the box, including (maybe even especially) the critics—we can design a world that truly benefits everyone. But be prepared, because that process may challenge that which we hold most dear.

Remoove the Sacred Cows

See what I did there? *Sacred cows*, if you don't know the term, are deeply ingrained beliefs, practices, or norms we rarely question, because they are considered beyond opposition. They can be personal—perhaps something significant, like moral boundaries, or just the firm opinion that mayonnaise should not exist as a condiment. Within organizations, they may take the form of rigid structures, a comfortable "that's how we've always done it" mindset, or an unchallenged cultural rule. In either case, because they are viewed as unassailable, sacred cows block shifts in perspective and hinder progress.

Like optical illusions, they condition us to see only what aligns with our expectations, making alternative perspectives invisible. They become so entrenched in personal and organizational identities that questioning them feels uncomfortable or risky. Yet, it's this discomfort that signals the opportunity for transformation.

Recognizing sacred cows begins with asking difficult but necessary questions: Why do we do things this way? Does this belief/behavior align with my values or goals? Who benefits? What makes it hard to challenge or question it? How does it affect outcomes? What might we gain by letting it go? The resulting moments of clarity expose the hidden dynamics shaping our behaviors and systems. By exposing the sacred cows and the assumptions behind them, we can begin to free ourselves from the unseen forces shaping our lives and move toward greater awareness and intentionality.

Choking on the Kool-Aid

An unwillingness to alter perceptions and processes can leave us with incorrect assumptions that pose a threat to ourselves and others. Sacred cows, left unchecked, can bring an organization to its knees. During my days working in the nonprofit sector, I once had a front-row seat to a story that I think will summarize my point in a nutshell.

Let me set the scene. This is the story of a CEO, a catastrophic misstep, and a powerful lesson in leadership. The CEO in question? Let's call him Marty. Marty was a very charismatic man and was very well thought of in the community. He was a self-proclaimed disruptor but unfortunately had, shall we say, a tenuous relationship with accountability and common sense. The sacred cow? A culture of compliance and fear that kept him untouchable. The leadership team and our board of directors had ill-advisedly built the altar to that bovine beast by sidestepping conflict, tiptoeing around his ego, and convincing ourselves that addressing his behaviors wasn't worth the fight.

Marty liked to sprinkle his speeches with jargon that he thought made him sound edgy. Chief among them: "sipping my own Kool-Aid." Yes, that was his favorite. If you knew this man, you'd understand. Strangely, he was kind of famous for using it. At every meeting, every event, everyone expected it. You couldn't stop him from slipping it in somewhere.

Fast-forward to a meeting in Washington, DC, with Congresswoman Jackie Speier. You might imagine, but let me reassure you, this was a big deal for our little nonprofit. A positive outcome could mean indefinite funding to help us meet the needs of those we served. The stakes were high, but we were prepared—or so we thought. If you've ever spent time on the Hill (though it's a solid practice for a meeting of any magnitude), you know you'd be remiss not to have a solid briefing packet that outlines not only your talking points, but also background information on who you will be sitting down with. We made sure that Marty had been fully briefed.

The energy in the room was serious, reflecting the weight of the occasion. As Marty finished outlining our mission and explained our request, he couldn't resist unleashing his signature catchphrase: "... but I'm not sure if I'm just sipping my own Kool-Aid." Time froze, and the air was immediately sucked out of the room. My eyes bulged. The words "Are you fucking kidding me?" flashed like a neon marquee across my mind (but I'm pretty sure I didn't say them out loud). The Congresswoman's staff looked like they'd seen a ghost. Marty, with all the self-awareness of a brick, didn't realize the tidal wave of discomfort he had unleashed.

For those of you who may be unfamiliar with the origins of that little phrase, it references the horrific 1978 Jonestown massacre where over nine hundred people died in a forced mass "suicide," many by having cyanide mixed into a certain grape-flavored beverage. Congresswoman Jackie Speier was a survivor of that tragedy.

"You *really* shouldn't say *that* to *me*," the Congresswoman calmly replied. With dignity and grace, she explained to Marty the specific nature of his profound fuck-up. Marty, of course, pled ignorance, swearing he had no idea. The meeting was over, and suffice it to say, we did not receive our funding. As we sheepishly gathered our things and headed out the door, the Congresswoman let loose with one last parting shot. "By the way ... it was Flavor Aid, not Kool-Aid."

I definitely added Marty to my burn book after that. I didn't go full Regina George. I didn't call him a "fugly slut" (or did I?). But he was absolutely memorialized as a cautionary tale of what leadership *shouldn't* look like. Sacred cows thrive on nice—on our collective decision to prioritize comfort over accountability. Our meeting with Congresswoman Speier wasn't just a correction; it was a mirror held up to our complicity in creating a culture where the sacred cows of ego and avoidance thrive. And that day, she gave Marty a perspective shift he hadn't asked for but desperately needed.

You may recall a moment when a shift in perspective was thrust upon you. Maybe it wasn't as terrible or embarrassing as our meeting on Capitol Hill. Maybe it was something more benign—like finding out that the rest of the world calls "soccer" football, that what we call "football" isn't even a thing anywhere else in the world, and that some of the assumptions you held about the universality of culture, and the dominance of American culture, were false. These moments remind us that the world is bigger than our own perspective. They help us recognize that our lens is not the only one and that there's always more to discover.

The Paradox of American Cynicism

Speaking of 'Murica, a sacred cow central to cultural understanding is the unspoken rule *don't rock the boat*—the belief that challenging norms or questioning silent social constructs is inherently rude or disruptive. This mindset upholds the status quo by discouraging deeper reflection on the invisible frameworks that guide our actions. However, I think it's safe to say that Americans also pride themselves on a healthy skepticism of authority. It's one of the few lessons we've learned that seems to apply across the board.

No matter what side of the aisle you fall on, we are quick to point out manipulation in politics, media, and foreign governments as we see it, labeling it as propaganda, corruption, or, yes, "fake news." More and more, we question the honesty of politicians and distrust institutions that overtly wield power. People are losing trust. A recent Edelman Trust Barometer report shows that only 40 percent of Americans believe the government makes fair and wise decisions.[6] Many feel that politics has become too divided, misinformation is everywhere, and leaders aren't solving big problems like inequality and public health.

This cynicism regarding our national structures is not limited to the political arena. Many people in the United States believe the system is unfair, no matter who is in charge. A 2024 study by the FrameWorks Institute found that 70 percent of Americans surveyed think powerful forces control how things work.[7] This belief is widespread across different political groups, with 72 percent of Republicans and 65 percent of Democrats agreeing that "the system is rigged." People of all backgrounds feel this way, including 75 percent of Black Americans, 71 percent of Latinx Americans, 72 percent of Asian Americans, and 65 percent of White Americans. The feeling also crosses income levels: 78 percent of those earning under $25,000 and 61 percent of those making over $150,000 say the system works against them. Nat Kendall-Taylor, CEO of the

FrameWorks Institute, says this belief is one of the most pervasive in all of American culture. It shapes how people think about money, politics, and fairness in society.

Americans may agree the system is unfair, but they don't always agree on who it hurts most. Just over half (56 percent) believe it works against Black and Brown communities, while the remaining 44 percent think it targets the White working class. These views are shaped by personal experiences and the stories people hear. The FrameWorks Institute warns that simply saying "the system is rigged" without context can lead to confusion, fear, or even harmful thinking. To create real change, we need to explain who benefits, who loses, and what can be done—not just point out the problem.

Surprisingly, according to the Trust Barometer report mentioned earlier, 53 percent of Americans trust *businesses* to do the right thing when it comes to justice. Similarly, 62 percent believe CEOs should help solve social issues, not just run their companies. This creates an interesting paradox—many people distrust the government but still have faith in corporations. That trust can make it harder to see how workplace culture shapes our behavior. While people easily recognize political manipulation, they may overlook how social norms—like avoiding conflict or keeping the peace—quietly influence their actions. The fear of speaking up, especially at work, keeps many people from intervening even when they see problems.

These insights show that where we place our trust affects how we act. While trust in government shifts, people often have more confidence in businesses, employers, and local institutions. This creates a chance for workplaces to balance respect with honest conversations, allowing real change, not just surface-level niceness. The goal is to make niceness a bridge to equity, not a barrier.

PROMISING PRACTICE 6
No Crying over Spilled Milk

(Get it?!? Because of the cows . . .)

As I noted at the beginning of this chapter, journaling has provided me with a unique space where I can connect the dots between strategy and emotion, action and reflection, enabling me to approach my experiences with greater awareness and intentionality. What began as a begrudging assignment revealed hidden patterns and shifted my thinking in ways I couldn't have anticipated. My initial resistance serves as a reflection of how uncomfortable change, even in small things, can feel.

Still, this exercise became a lifelong practice—proving that even tools we're skeptical of can be transformative when approached with curiosity and consistency. To cultivate awareness, challenge assumptions, and inspire fresh perspectives as you continue your journey, I invite you to observe opportunities for perspective shifts in your daily life (including a reflection on any sacred cows) so you can uncover opportunities to reimagine what you think, feel, and do.

I'm giving you the exact instructions I received in 2013. Please try this practice for at least four weeks—I think you'll be amazed!

Instructions for Your Creative Journal

Commit to daily entries

Make **one entry every day** describing something you noticed that you had not observed before.

Include one observation aligned with the **weekly focus topics**.

Weekly focus topics

Week One: Systems & Processes

a. Observe systems or processes that are effective and those that are not.

b. **Reflect:** What makes the good ones work? How could the bad ones improve?

Week Two: Progress & Growth

a. Identify things you can do now that you couldn't do three years ago.

b. **Reflect:** What factors enabled this growth? How do they connect to your personal or professional journey?

Week Three: Fresh Perspectives

a. Intentionally go somewhere unfamiliar or view something from a new perspective.

b. **Reflect:** What stood out? Why do you think you hadn't noticed this before?

Week Four: Connect Insights to Sacred Cows

a. Choose one observation or insight from your journal each day.

b. Link it to one of your sacred cows—long-held beliefs, assumptions, or "nice" behaviors that may no longer serve you.

c. **Reflect:** What would happen if you challenged or let go of this sacred cow?

(CONTINUED)

Example Journal Entry (Week Four)

- **Observation:** During a team meeting, I realized I often avoid directly disagreeing with others, choosing neutral language instead.

- **Sacred cow connection:** I've been conditioned to believe that avoiding conflict maintains harmony. This "niceness" has led to miscommunications and stalled progress.

- **Reflection:** If I let go of this sacred cow, I could replace it with clear, constructive communication, prioritizing respect over fear of disagreement.

Your creative journal (a.k.a. "burn book") isn't about tearing things down—it's about burning away what no longer serves you. By the end of this exercise, you'll have a clearer view of the illusions, sacred cows, and invisible norms shaping your decisions. And once you start seeing the illusions for what they are, you won't just question the rules—you'll rewrite them.

6

Dancing
with the Devil

As your perceptions shift, so will your understanding of the world, which can be unsettling. That's okay. Discomfort is part of the process, but resolution will come. You'll reassess long-held beliefs and question what you once took for granted.

Heroes and Villains

My husband loves superhero movies—Marvel Cinematic Universe, Spiderman, Superman, DC ... or whatever (clearly, I pay close attention). But his favorite character is Batman. During one of his gazillion rewatches, a line from *The Dark Knight* caught my attention. In this scene, Harvey Dent (Aaron Eckhart) is at dinner with Bruce Wayne (Christian Bale), and their dates, discussing Batman's role in Gotham City.

Harvey says, "You either die a hero, or you live long enough to see yourself become the villain." It made me wonder—where is the line between hero and villain? Who gets to decide? And what do those titles really mean? Here's how I break down those roles:

- ***For the good of all mankind.*** Many people, when asked to name a hero, might pick a celebrity, politician, sports star, or author. I define a hero as someone who acts without the promise of personal benefit or the chance to witness the impact of their efforts. They take action for people they may never meet, for causes that may never directly affect them, and at a cost they may not easily afford.

- ***Some people just want to watch the world burn.*** Villains are the antagonists no one admires. Their actions serve little purpose beyond self-aggrandizement, driven by an insatiable need for power, control, or personal gain. They see the world as something to exploit, relationships as tools to manipulate, and community as something to divide, leaving harm and chaos in their wake.

Good versus evil. Light versus dark. Justice versus the systems that perpetuate inequity. But what happens when someone who seems complicit in the very system we're questioning starts challenging it themselves?

Did We Just Become Best Friends!?!

In 2024, I attended the Forbes Power Women's Summit. It was a packed day, full of powerful women from every walk of life. One of the opening interviews featured Gwyneth Paltrow. I wasn't sure how much what she had to say would resonate with me. I may or may not have (but definitely did) rolled my eyes.

As a Black woman who has spent her career challenging entrenched systems, I've always been keenly aware of how differently the world treats White women. Gwyneth, a Hollywood star who happens to be the daughter of an actress and a Hollywood producer, has undeniably benefited from entrenched power structures. I don't mention that to diminish her talent. I only mean to point out that she is someone whose life has been laden with unearned advantages. And one of the perks of privilege is that you are often given the benefit of the doubt.

She can make mistakes, speak freely, and hold controversial beliefs—yet still be seen as well-meaning, just a bit naive. When Goop faced backlash for pseudoscience, the fallout was minimal, and her image remained intact. If a Black woman promoted vaginal steaming, NASA energy stickers, or jade eggs, the response wouldn't be so kind. We don't get to be "naive" or "eccentric"—we face skepticism, judgment, and outright hostility.

I walked into that room with these thoughts swirling.

Gwyneth opened by speaking about her love for Margaret Mead, the famous anthropologist. Mead often described how women *transmute*, forcing themselves to fit molds they never designed. This stood out because I'd written something similar after witnessing the contortionist act Justice Ketanji Brown Jackson put on during her 2022 Senate Judiciary Committee hearings, about the struggle Black women face in meeting unspoken and intentionally unattainable ideals.

Okay. So far, so good. But things will go off the rails at some point, right?

She followed up by offering advice: "Go toward discomfort, straight on. Just go for it." She emphasized that difficult conversations are the ones worth having because they make us grow. Her message: When fear or discomfort arises, lean into it.

I found myself nodding, but still had my guard up.

And then, she shared a story that immediately struck me. She'd switched her children to a gluten-, dairy-, and sugar-free diet due to one of the children's medical needs. But instead of

praise for putting her family's health first, she faced overwhelm-
ing backlash. She was called a bad mother, among many other
names not worth repeating. Some went so far as to suggest that
Child Protective Services should be called on her for "denying"
her children gluten and dairy. Can you imagine?

Once again, Gwyneth became a lightning rod for ridicule—
not for pseudoscience, but for making informed choices about
her child's health. Choices others didn't agree with or bother to
understand. Choices made with the input of doctors, parents,
and health experts. Choices she had every right to make.

Gwyneth is often dismissed as just a "pretty actress," and the
world seemed to prefer her in that role. But what made me sit up
that day was her take on why it happened. She said, "I don't want
to sound like a conspiracy theorist, but I've come to understand
that the entrenched systems of capitalism will punish you for
asking questions and challenging the status quo."

*Wait—what? Is this the same lady who used to be married to
the Coldplay guy? Named her daughter Apple?* Shakespeare in
Love? *Pepper freaking Potts? Who is now talking about systems
of capitalism?!?*

I was pleasantly surprised. Her experience echoed ideas in
this book—even the price of not playing nice. She credited those
who helped her see these systems more clearly and recognized
the responsibility we all share to push back. As she spoke of her
evolving understanding, I wondered who the voices shaping
her views were and felt encouraged. Just saying—if she needs
another voice of reason in her life, I'm available. Got her number?

It was refreshing—a reminder that even the people you least
expect can be impacted by, and help dismantle, oppressive
structures. While Gwenyth's motivation may not stem from a
shared understanding of anti-Blackness, I'm open to being
wrong. Her foundation is a starting point, and I'm willing to hold
space for it—because traditional power-holding groups are far

more likely to embrace this message of change from a pretty, blonde-haired, blue-eyed actress than from me.

And here she was, talking about something I've dedicated my career to: helping people see the harmful, entrenched systems we are forced to operate within and equipping them with the tools to challenge and disrupt those systems. Sitting there, I found that I had seamlessly transitioned from nodding skeptically to fully agreeing with her. It was also a reminder that all of us, including myself, must constantly check our assumptions and biases.

I often encounter disbelief about inequity—people are mystified that it's not just a distant issue affecting marginalized groups. Diversity isn't just for Black, Brown, disabled, or LGBTQIA+ people. It impacts everyone—even White people. You'd be surprised (or not) how many fail to see how inequity affects them personally. But entrenched systems that harm one group don't leave others unscathed. We may not have created the problem, but it's on all of us to correct it.

Society's message is clear: *Shut up, sit pretty, and play nice.* But that day, Gwyneth freaking Paltrow reminded us that real power lies in owning who you are. Her words showed that even those far removed from these conversations can wake up to how power works. In a room full of women leaders, her story was a call to stop playing nice and start getting real about what it takes to be a hero.

She didn't overthrow capitalism that day and may never fully grasp what many of us fight for. But even in privileged spaces that uphold inequity, cracks are forming. And if she can start questioning them, maybe others will, too.

Am I the Asshole Here?

A popular Reddit thread, #AITAH is a very interesting sociological experiment that questions the nature of our interactions. But for me, it also resonated with a truth that I had long sensed but resisted acknowledging. Wrestling with self-doubt, the lesson came slowly: *Sometimes, to be the hero, I would have to be the villain in someone else's story.*

I began my career as a communicator and fundraiser in the nonprofit sector with clear eyes and a full heart. I wanted to help people, have a meaningful impact on the world, and be an agent of sustainable change in a system that desperately needed it. Little did I know the hoops I would have to jump through to fund that change. Far removed from the philanthropic ideal I had imagined, I found the mission itself overshadowed as I navigated a labyrinth of social expectations and unspoken rules.

For me, the disillusionment began when I encountered the "ladies who lunch" for the first time. Have you ever come across these "ladies"? I remember thinking it seemed like a fairly ridiculous designation when I first heard it. I thought, "Who the fuck doesn't eat lunch?" Unbeknownst to me, this phrase represented a rarefied species—a unique breed that thrives in high society's country club dining rooms. These women are as essential to the charity ecosystem as bees are to pollination, fluttering from one luncheon to the next, spreading gossip, glitter, and the gospel of giving.

Attending my first lunch with them was an experience I'll never forget. I was a deer caught in the headlights of Chanel-clad doyennes armed with Birkin bags and steely determination. The room buzzed with a melodic mix of pleasantries and veiled barbs, the proprietary language of these "ladies": "Oh darling, you look fabulous! Did you finally get that Botox?" or "Your new Jaguar is simply divine, but isn't it a bit much after the divorce?" Every compliment was a double-edged sword, as sharp as their Jimmy Choo stilettos.

The lunch was held at an exclusive venue where the salads cost more than my car payment. I felt like an undercover agent infiltrating a secret society, half expecting them to ask me for a password. But as the meal went on, I began to understand the power behind the facade. Lunch was not just a meal; it was an event, a strategic operation, a power play wrapped in cashmere and served with a side of arugula. It was a chance to network, to influence, and to make epic shit happen.

With impeccably matched pearls and perfectly coiffed hair that defied both gravity and the passage of time, these unsung heroines of high society wielded their wealth and influence with the precision of a surgeon and the flair of a Broadway star. A fortune could be raised with a flutter of eyelashes. I watched in awe as these grand dames of generosity waltzed through the social minefield with the grace of ballerinas and the cunning of chess grandmasters. They had a way of making you feel like the most important person in the world while simultaneously reminding you that you could never, ever be their equal.

For all their saccharine sweetness, I couldn't shake the feeling of being an outsider—a necessary outsider, sure, but an outsider nonetheless. To these women—these polished, primped, and proper paragons of society—we were the faceless staff, the invisible hands that made their charity events sparkle, the unseen gears in their well-oiled social machine. And the people we were actually there to raise money for? They were even more invisible, mere props in the benevolent theater, trotted out for photo ops and then forgotten the moment the cameras stopped rolling.

Navigating this surreal world of pastel power suits and diamond-studded determination would require me to perform a delicate dance of my own—a game of platitudes and pleasantries where one misstep might send these powerful women, and their checkbooks, running away. I had to suck it up and be "nice."

A Personal Reflection

Those years were a mix of hope and frustration. As nonprofit staff, we were deeply committed to our mission—feeding the hungry, sheltering the unhoused, and amplifying unheard voices. Yet, we spent too much time indulging wealthy donors, catering to their whims, and playing by their rules. Looking back, I wonder if we gave away too much of our power.

We saw them as necessary evils, believing their approval would fund our mission. With wealth, influence, and connections, they had the power to create real change. But their obsession with image and status reduced every noble cause to just another social event. What if we had been direct instead of bending over backward to be nice? Looking back, I see the missed opportunities when we should have pushed back—when we should have said, "Your image isn't the priority. The work, the people, the lives we're changing are." Instead, we tiptoed around their egos.

We let real change be stifled by the need to play nice, conforming to a world that valued appearances over substance. If I could do it again, I'd demand action without coddling or pretense. We didn't need their approval—we needed their commitment.

Maybe if we had stood our ground, we would have seen the change we fought so hard for. And what's worse? I learned that hardly any of the funds these ladies raised actually went to programs—the bulk of the money funded their lavish parties and fashion shows, with only a minuscule percentage making its way back to the communities in need. I was floored by the absurdity of it all, questioning why extravagance was a prerequisite for generosity.

My experience became a cautionary tale of how easily their trivial concerns overshadowed our critical work. But it also taught me this: Sometimes, you must risk the wrath of those in power. If you don't, you'll keep bending to their will, losing sight of what matters—or worse, losing yourself. In their world, they were the heroes—graceful benefactors, saviors of the less fortunate. But if challenging their performative philanthropy would make me the villain, maybe that was a title worth embracing.

The Villainy of Nice

This isn't just a story about the opulence of the "ladies who lunch." It's about social conditioning, control, and the illusion of progress—endless talk, empty meetings, and polite smiles masking deep frustration.

The real issue is our reluctance to dissent, disrupt, and challenge the established norms—vital actions for bringing about real change. I share this story not just for its absurdity, but because it reflects a larger myth: that being nice, keeping the peace, and avoiding conflict will create progress. It won't. Nice is a comfort zone that silences truth, a false measure of progress, and a tool of complacency.

You may not have faced this exact drama, but I bet you've had moments where you wished you'd spoken up, acted differently, or pushed back. That's the point. Disrupting the norms we've been conditioned to accept takes conscious, deliberate action—but at what cost?

PROMISING PRACTICE 7
Reframe It Like You Mean It

Asset-based framing helps us focus on strengths and opportunities instead of problems. It doesn't ignore unfairness but challenges negative thinking. By looking at things differently, we can rethink our reactions, grow, and turn tough moments into opportunities for real change—just like

(CONTINUED)

when I unexpectedly agreed with Gwyneth Paltrow at the Forbes Power Women's Summit.

Here are four ways we can use asset-based framing to reframe our skepticism and discomfort into insight:

Don't be (too) suspicious.

I nodded as Gwyneth described how women are conditioned to conform—something I've experienced my whole life, though from a different vantage point. My first instinct was to dismiss her perspective because of her privilege. But reframing it, I saw her privilege as a tool—her voice reaching audiences who might never hear mine. Her story became a gateway to deeper conversations about systemic inequities.

Face the funk.

When she said, "Go toward discomfort, straight on," I felt it. Discomfort signals something important—something worth addressing. My first instinct was to resist admitting she had a point. Instead, I embraced it as a chance to learn, connect, and grow. Her words were a reminder: Real change comes from leaning into discomfort, so we can work toward resolution.

Find the thread.

Gwyneth's story of the backlash over her parenting choices struck a chord. Our experiences differ, but the pattern was familiar—society punishes women, especially those who challenge norms. Instead of dismissing her struggle, I saw it as proof that entrenched power resists disruption, no matter who questions it. This shift helped me connect her experience to the larger fight for equity and inclusion, bridging the gap between our seemingly different worlds.

Tag, you're it!

When Gwyneth called out capitalism for punishing those who challenge the status quo, I had a realization: Her privilege wasn't a barrier—it was a tool. At first, I thought, "She's irrelevant to this conversation." But reframing it, I again saw the opportunity—she could reach people who'd never listen to me, shifting narratives in ways I couldn't alone.

By using asset-based framing, I went from doubt to connection, seeing Gwyneth's privilege as a tool, not a barrier. This approach helps us turn discomfort into chances to challenge systems, build connections, and create change. It encourages us to pause, reflect, and respond in ways that open doors for teamwork, new ideas, and progress—even in unexpected places.

PART III

DO

7

Status Update:
It's Complicated

$\mathbb{A}$s you move along the Nice to Nerve Continuum, the focus shifts from feelings and perceptions to action. Now that we're aligned, it's time to, in the words of the Greek goddess of victory, *"Just do it."* Let's explore what that means and how to put it into practice.

Not Too Hot, Not Too Cold, Just Problematic

Throughout this journey, I've embraced a core belief: Question everything and everyone. Seeking answers is essential to understanding the world and imagining change. Building on the last chapter, we must now ask: What if everything I've been taught about heroes and villains is flawed? Am I meant to root for the villains now?

Do you remember when you first learned about heroes and villains? Maybe not a specific moment, but likely through childhood stories like *The Three Little Pigs*. The lesson is clear: the Big Bad Wolf is a threat, willing to destroy anything in his way—good versus evil, simple enough. But now, consider *Goldilocks and the Three Bears*. On the surface, it seems harmless, but what if there's more to it than meets the eye?

In the story, Goldilocks (our young protagonist) stumbles upon a house in the woods belonging to a family of bears who are out for a morning walk. Finding no one home, she helps herself to their food, chairs, and beds, assuming availability grants her entitlement. When discovered, she screams and flees, framing the bears as the aggressors—though they've done nothing wrong. (Perhaps this is also our first lesson in how *Karens* operate—am I right?!)

Step back—who's the real villain here? Goldilocks commits felony breaking and entering, with potential charges of theft and property damage, though likely reduced to misdemeanor trespassing. Let's be real—a judge would never throw the book at Blondie. In many states, the bears could have legally defended their home with force. Yet, the story never suggests Goldilocks is at fault. The story ends there, but what happens next? Maybe Goldilocks learns a lesson about crime—or maybe she runs back to her village, claiming she was attacked by bears. Enraged, the townspeople hunt them down. It wouldn't be the first time in history that a White girl's lies led to grave injustice.

Of course, this is just a fairy tale. But if even children's tales blur the lines between heroes and villains, what hope do we have? Maybe the real lesson is: *It's complicated.*

I would like to help us solve for this by proposing a third classification: the *antihero*. Not the hero we deserve, but the one we need. Our world isn't black and white—it's full of gray areas where multiple truths coexist, demanding a more nuanced perspective. An antihero acts out of necessity rather than altruism. Though perhaps not inherently driven by virtue, they navigate the messy middle ground to step up when others won't, confronting challenges head-on. Imperfect yet resolute, the anti-hero is a flawed but willing participant in the pursuit of progress.

In a world that values order over justice, those who dare to disrupt the current order are labeled as the villains of the story. Instead, I suggest that we embrace the role of the antihero. Anti-heroes are catalysts for progress. They question the established order and force others to confront uncomfortable truths. In comic books, the antihero often utilizes questionable methods to achieve their goals. But taking on this role is not about causing harm; I am not giving you permission to act out of pocket. The difference is, *our actions will be righteous, but society will tell us they are wrong.*

Goldilocks's isn't the only story that needs rethinking. Throughout history, many change agents have been unfairly cast as villains simply for rejecting the way things are. Yet their defiance, their willingness to disrupt and challenge injustice, is exactly what makes them heroes—or rather, *antiheroes*—today.

On the Shoulders of Giants

I often reflect on the change agents who came before me and how their narratives are told. Over time, their stories are frequently sanitized to make their radical actions more palatable to those who fear dissent and disruption. When it comes down to it, simply daring to be yourself in a system committed to social control and complacency is a villainous act. Refusing to conform to expectations, especially when those expectations are unjust, is a powerful act of resistance.

Martin Luther King Jr. embodied that spirit of defiance. He recognized that change demands more than polite requests and adherence to social norms. Today, more than ever, his incisive critique of "the absence of tensions" as an impediment to justice resonates with me. In his "Letter from the Birmingham City Jail," Dr. King identified a sobering truth: that the most significant obstacle to freedom for the Black community was not the overt hostility of White supremacists. As he wrote:

> *The Negro's great stumbling block in his stride toward free-dom is not the White Citizen's Councilor or the Ku Klux Klan-ner, but the white moderate, who is more devoted to "order" than to justice; who prefers a negative peace which is the absence of tension to a positive peace which is the presence of justice; who constantly says: "I agree with you in the goal you seek, but I cannot agree with your methods of direct action"; who paternalistically believes he can set the timeta-ble for another man's freedom; who lives by a mythical con-cept of time and who constantly advises the Negro to wait for a "more convenient season."*[1]

He knew that order was not the measure of justice. The uncomfortable reality is that these moderates, while outwardly condemning injustice, will retreat into silence if it threatens their privilege and status. Unfortunately, the words that Dr. King wrote in his jail cell in 1963 still ring true today.

Just as White moderates sought to uphold a superficial peace by avoiding direct confrontation with racial injustice, the fetishization of "niceness" in contemporary society can serve as a means of maintaining a semblance of order while indefinitely delaying uncomfortable conversations about privilege, power, and systemic oppression.

These days, Dr. King is lionized, appropriated as a means of critiquing present-day activism. His image is a beacon of civil-ity, an uncontroversial monument to peaceful and passive pro-test. Never mind that he was arrested thirty times and that polls at the time showed that he was hated by a majority of Ameri-cans—not to mention the pesky detail that he was assassinated.

As Dr. King aptly noted, an individual has not started living until he can rise above the narrow confines of his individualistic concerns to the broader concerns of all humanity.[2] Promoting politeness and civility as virtues encourages individuals to prioritize the comfort of the privileged majority over the urgent needs of marginalized communities—discouraging dissent rather than challenging entrenched systems of oppression.

Why Disruption Alone Isn't the Vibe

In the end, it's those willing to disrupt the forces of complacency that drive progress. Whether seen as villains or heroes, they are the catalysts of change. But disruption is the starting line, not the conclusion. It is incomplete and, dare I say, naive as a singular notion. Disruption exposes inequities and challenges accepted norms, but after the dust settles, no benevolent overseer is waiting to ensure progress takes root.

Imagine a single progressive company—Ben & Jerry's, for example—known for its unapologetic commitment to smashing the patriarchy, dismantling White supremacy, and championing social justice. Its stance is commendable, its actions necessary, and its mere existence in corporate America noteworthy. However, one company standing against outdated systems cannot change the broader rules in our economic, political, and cultural structures.

There is only us.

This world, with all its flaws, injustices, and potential, is ours to break or build. Our progress can be charted in the systems we design, the stories we tell, and the legacies we leave.

Somebody Get This Lion a Pen!

The African proverb "Until the lion tells his side of the story, the tale of the hunt will always glorify the hunter" reminds us that traditional narratives uphold power structures. Counter-narratives are more than storytelling—they are tools of disruption and empowerment. By reframing dominant narratives, they expose bias and inequity, forcing uncomfortable truths into focus. They challenge the status quo and provide agency to marginalized communities, allowing them to define their realities and reclaim their power.[3]

For change agents, using counter-narratives means demanding accountability and inspiring action. Counter-narratives not only illuminate the gaps in dominant stories but also provide a road map for justice by centering the lived experiences of those most affected by oppression.

Not All Antiheroes Wear Capes

Another real-life "giant," Shirley Chisholm was the first Black woman elected to Congress and, in 1972, became the first woman to seek the Democratic nomination for president. Her campaign, known as the "Chisholm Trail," boldly challenged a system steeped in sexism and racism and unapologetically claimed space in a political landscape that sought to exclude her. Blocked from televised debates, she was forced to fight legal battles to secure even a single speaking opportunity. She faced relentless resistance, including assassination attempts, yet refused to be silenced.[4]

Chisholm's iconic statement, "If they don't give you a seat at the table, bring a folding chair," embodies her defiance and determination. It wasn't just a call to demand change but an invitation to create it. She was a visionary leader who confronted head-on the reality of making space for voices like hers.

Shirley Chisholm reminds us that meaningful progress often requires telling your own stories, forcing systems of power to reckon with your presence and possibility. Reflecting on her legacy, she said, "I want history to remember me . . . not as the first Black woman to make a bid for the presidency of the United States, but as a Black woman who lived in the 20th century and dared to be herself. I want to be remembered as a catalyst for change in America."[5] Her story compels us not just to celebrate resilience but to confront the systemic racism and sexism that demand it.

I've Said It before, and I'll Say It Again...

Words shape worlds. Remember in the Introduction, when I said that this book was written to my fellow comms professionals? The tools at our disposal have the ability to change minds and influence behaviors in both our present and our future. When we say all behavior is communication, we mean that every action, choice, and societal norm is influenced by the stories we tell and the messages we reinforce. Strategic communication can transform ideas into actions and actions into lasting change.

How, you ask? Allow me to share.

In the 1920s, breakfast in America was typically light. But the Beech-Nut Packing Company, a significant bacon producer, wanted to boost sales and turned to Edward Bernays (the "Father of Public Relations") for a solution.

Rather than launching a straightforward ad campaign, Bernays took a more psychological and strategic approach. He gathered endorsements from several thousand physicians, promoting the idea that a robust breakfast was the cornerstone of good health, essential for energy and productivity. He then cleverly advertised this "hearty breakfast" to include bacon and eggs, presenting it as the most beneficial way to start the day.[6]

Bernays turned what was essentially a marketing ploy into a cultural norm. Today, the notion that a "traditional" American morning meal consists of bacon and eggs goes unquestioned—just "part of our balanced breakfast." But it resulted from a carefully crafted communication strategy. Bernays didn't just sell a product; he revolutionized how we started our day, selling an idea that influenced behavior for generations. Ever been told that "breakfast is the most important meal of the day"? Now you know why.

Still don't believe me? Maybe Bernays got lucky...

In the mid-1980s, Texas faced a serious problem: litter. Highways were cluttered with trash, and efforts to address the issue through traditional messaging had largely failed. Enter the phrase "Don't Mess with Texas." Instead of focusing on guilt or environmental responsibility, the campaign appealed to Texans' sense of pride, toughness, and independence. Suddenly, throwing trash on the highway wasn't just inconsiderate—it was un-Texan.

The phrase debuted on billboards, in TV ads, and on bumper stickers. It was delivered by iconic Texan musicians like Stevie Ray Vaughan and actors who embodied Texan grit. And it worked. Within four years, roadside litter had decreased by 72 percent.[7] The phrase, a simple anti-littering message, evolved into a widely recognized symbol of Texan pride, used far beyond its original context. It's a testament to how the right message, framed in culturally resonant language, can transform behavior on a massive scale.

With great power comes great responsibility.

In the 1970s, sidewalks were inaccessible to people who used wheelchairs. Disability rights activists fought for curb cuts— small ramps at sidewalk corners—to make public spaces more inclusive.[8] Critics argued that the effort and expense weren't justified for such a niche need.

However, once curb cuts were installed, the benefits were found to extend far beyond the disabled community. Parents with strollers, travelers with rolling suitcases, workers with delivery carts, joggers—everyone found curb cuts incredibly useful. These days, they're just a part of our daily existence. You may not have given them a second thought before this moment.

These developments led to the recognition of a sociological phenomenon that came to be known as the "curb-cut effect," illustrating a profound truth: When we design with the most marginalized in mind, we create solutions that benefit everyone. This principle now influences policy and design far beyond sidewalks, informing practices in technology, education, and workplace culture. The curb cut didn't just change infrastructure; it changed how we perceive accessibility and inclusion.[9]

Applying the Power of Communication to Drive Change

The cartoon *Captain Planet* taught a generation of kids to reduce, reuse, and recycle. The *Got Milk?* campaign made drinking dairy sexy. Need I go on? These stories highlight a key insight: Communication isn't just about exchanging information. It's about shaping how people see the world and choose to act within it. The words, phrases, and symbols we use are far more than semantics; they are tools of influence and transformation. Stories like the ones I've shared here demonstrate that purposeful change doesn't happen accidentally. It is crafted through deliberate messaging, strategic positioning, and the courage to challenge what exists today—and it is woven into every aspect of our lives.

In our workplaces, the backlash against DEI initiatives is real and growing. This momentum has been emboldened by the 2025 Trump administration, which has actively dismantled federal DEI programs, most notably by signing executive orders to eliminate what it calls "radical and wasteful" DEI efforts across the entire government and removing DEI from Foreign Service promotion criteria.[10] (Not to mention absurdly blaming anything and everything on DEI as the default. Plane crashes after we fired a bunch of air traffic safety people? Must've been DEI . . . yet I digress . . .) To counter it, we must go beyond superficial messaging and adopt bold, strategic communication that positions DEI as fundamental to organizational health and success. Instead of generic platitudes, communicate how teams prioritizing diversity drive innovation, profitability, and employee satisfaction. Show data, but also tell stories that humanize the impact of inclusion.

If your company prides itself on excellence, integrity, or innovation, position DEI as an integral part of that identity. Make it clear that failing to embrace diversity is failing to live up to the company's own standards. Be willing to confront resistance directly. Use language that doesn't just "invite" inclusion but demands accountability. Avoid the trap of polite, noncommittal messaging. Instead, clearly communicate the expectation: "We are an inclusive workplace, and we all share the responsibility to uphold that."

In our communities, we can use communication to mobilize people toward collective action and challenge systemic issues like racism, environmental injustice, and economic inequality. Community campaigns work when they tap into shared values. For example, frame environmental action as a way to protect local heritage or ensure a better future for children. Appeal to pride, responsibility, and identity rather than guilt or fear.

Emphasize that advocating for marginalized groups benefits everyone. When communities invest in accessible public spaces, fair housing, or equitable policies, the benefits ripple outward. Make it clear that equity is not a zero-sum game; it's a win for the entire community. Don't shy away from naming injustices and calling out those who enable them. Create messaging that asks people to show solidarity through action, not just words.

Change starts at home, where the values we reinforce shape the next generation. Design family norms and practices that are inclusive and supportive for everyone. Communicate that standing up for oneself or others is not only acceptable but expected. Show children that advocating for fairness benefits the whole family unit.

Be intentional about the stories and narratives you share. Talk about historical and personal examples that give children permission to set boundaries and defend themselves. Communicate that protecting one's dignity and integrity is more important than maintaining superficial peace. Teach that kindness is valuable, but not when it comes at the expense of justice or self-respect.

In personal relationships, genuine connection and growth come from honest communication and the willingness to hold ourselves and others accountable. Frame difficult conversations around shared values and respect. For example, if a friend or family member says something harmful, addressing it isn't being mean—it honors the values of honesty and integrity within the relationship.

Be strategic in how you present feedback or boundaries. Craft your message in a way that resonates with the other person's worldview. Effective communication isn't just about what you say, but how you frame it to be heard. But be willing to say the hard things—authenticity preserves trust. Communicate clearly: "I care about this relationship, which is why I'm being direct with you." Remember, accountability is an act of care, not cruelty.

The Mandate: "Have Nerve, Even if It's Not Nice"

Change requires us to communicate with intention, clarity, and courage. Communication shapes behavior, culture, and norms.

But to drive the change we seek, we must be willing to disrupt comfort, challenge assumptions, and reject complacency.

Niceness may smooth the edges, but it rarely shifts the ground beneath us. Nerve bends the moral arc, tips the scales of justice, and creates a world where progress is not just possible, but achievable—because we choose to make it so.

PROMISING PRACTICE 8
Clap Back with Narrative

By using counter-narratives, individuals can

- Shift the focus from maintaining comfort to pursuing justice.
- Challenge dominant systems of power and privilege.
- Empower marginalized communities to define their own stories.
- Create spaces for authentic, inclusive dialogue that fosters accountability and action.

Mastering counter-narratives can provide the courage to disrupt the status quo and the clarity to envision and build a more equitable future. Here are some tips to keep in mind:

- **Identify the dominant narrative:** Recognize the prevailing story that upholds the status quo. For example, dominant narratives often paint activists like Martin Luther King Jr. as "peaceful" to diminish the radical nature of their work and are likely to sanitize Shirley Chisholm's campaigns to emphasize resilience while ignoring systemic barriers.

- **Center marginalized voices:** Present stories from those whose perspectives are commonly excluded. This requires creating platforms for people on the margins to speak for themselves rather than having their stories filtered through the lens of dominant groups.

- **Expose structural inequities:** Use the counter-narrative to highlight how systems of power create and sustain inequities. For example, Chisholm's struggle to be included in presidential debates and her resilience in the face of assassination attempts can be framed to show the systemic barriers Black women face in political leadership.

- **Reclaim power through storytelling:** Share counter-narratives that emphasize agency and defiance, reframing marginalization as a source of strength. Instead of focusing solely on Chisholm's "folding chair" metaphor, highlight how she demanded structural change by taking legal action to participate in debates.

- **Foster dialogue and action:** Counter-narratives are not just about exposing truths; they also pave the way for accountability and systemic change. Use them to invite others into conversations about dismantling oppressive structures and creating equitable solutions.[11]

8

Sweat the
Small Stuff

A year or so ago, I came across a quote by author Jay Kristoff: "An avalanche starts with one pebble. A forest with one seed. And it takes one word to make the whole world stop and listen. All you need is the right one."[1] Living up to the impact of Martin Luther King Jr. may seem out of reach. Changing cultural paradigms like Edward Bernays is a daunting task. But these larger-than-life legacies are built on smaller, intentional actions.

Confronting Everyday Derailments

Storytime! I was sitting at my desk one morning, coffee in hand, with one eye on a team meeting that could have been an email, when I stumbled upon an Instagram reel highlighting a study conducted by professors from Harvard, Boston University, and MIT. The findings weren't surprising, but seeing the facts laid out in hard data—numbers, bar graphs, charts—was validating and infuriating. I thought, "There are not enough people talking about this!"

The study examined coworker demographics in predominantly White workspaces, which affected the retention and promotion of Black, Asian, and Hispanic employees. I saw my own experiences, and those of countless other marginalized individuals, reflected in the data. The numbers were grim: Black new hires had a 32 percent higher turnover rate and were 26 percent less likely to be promoted on time than White counterparts. Black women had it the worst, with a 51 percent higher turnover rate than White women.[2] The findings confirmed what we've known for years: Despite being *twice as good*, we're still getting *half as much*.

I summarized the takeaways and shared the study on LinkedIn, determined to spark a conversation. I wanted people to see the truth—not just in anecdotes or stories, but in cold, hard facts. I wrote:

> *The effect of white coworkers on Black women's careers has been detrimental. Harvard's study confirms it. I'm not saying, "I told you so." Harvard University is. Black women have been calling out these issues for years. The behaviors we see from white coworkers aren't isolated incidents or aberrations. They're part of a pattern. And yet, here we are—still being asked to explain why we're exhausted.*

The post picked up traction. There was a mix of supportive comments, shares, and personal reflections. Then, I felt a familiar knot tighten in my stomach as if on cue, a comment came that shifted the energy in a way I'd been bracing for.

"I've been laid off twice," this woman wrote, *"and my dad lost his job last year. It's hard for everyone, no matter how we look."*

I leaned back in my chair and sighed. Here we go. She hadn't directly refuted the data, but she'd done something just as damaging—redirected the conversation, taking the focus off Black women's experiences and making it about herself. And then there was that kicker: *"no matter how we look."*

It was one of those dismissive phrases, often said with the best intention. It's the same sentiment behind "I don't see color" or "We should hire based on merit." It's language that erases the unique challenges marginalized people face by flattening everything into a one-size-fits-all hardship.

I wasn't angry, just exhausted—again. Here was this meticulously researched study outlining the systemic barriers that Black women face in the workplace, barriers we've shouted into the void about for literally centuries, and someone dared to come along and say, "Hey, we all struggle. What's the big deal?" Ironically, it was a perfect, real-time example of the behaviors the study warns about.

I stared at the screen, feeling the weight of her comment, deciding how to respond. I could've ignored her, but I knew that wouldn't sit right with me. Her comment derailed the conversation, yes, but now I had an opportunity to steer it back—and cement a teachable moment. I started typing...

"You missed the assignment," I began. "The conversation was about systemic barriers disproportionately affecting Black professionals' retention and promotion. Yes, unemployment is hard. I hear you—it's tough, and no one is downplaying how stressful job loss can be. But let's not confuse the issue."

I paused, rereading my words. I wanted to be firm. I had no intention of sugarcoating.

"Empowerment isn't something we just 'find' on our own—systems either help or hurt that process. While we can advocate for fair wages and address inequity simultaneously, let's not sidestep the core issue. We weren't talking about layoffs; we're talking about a system that places invisible walls in front of Black professionals, particularly Black women, even when we have the skills, talent, and qualifications to succeed. Systemic barriers have held Black people back for 400+ years, and no amount of personal hardship will erase the need to have honest conversations about racial inequity."

I hit the reply button and waited for what might happen next.

And then the floodgates opened. Many "co-conspirators" (my preferred descriptor over "ally") took it upon themselves to gently, or not so gently, challenge this woman. One follower commented that my responses were "a full-on lesson plan."

I felt relieved (and, admittedly, proud); I'd managed to get the conversation back on track. And yet, the thought of how fantastically typical this situation was kept gnawing at me. Countless conversations about systemic inequities derail when someone centers their own experience, drawing false equivalencies between personal struggles and institutional barriers.

Too often, "nice" is used to keep conversations comfortable for those unaffected by the harm being discussed. In this case, the woman's well-meaning attempt to find common ground sidetracked and diluted the conversation. Niceness, in the face of hard truths, becomes erasure. Her effort to "add layers" wasn't just misguided; it was the kind of *all lives matter* deflection that prevents us from addressing the specific challenges Black women and other marginalized communities continue to face.

Or, colloquially, "Save the rainforest doesn't mean fuck all the other trees." If you want to discuss layoffs and their impact on the general population, go ahead—on your own page, in your own space. But don't hijack a conversation meant to address the unique systemic barriers Black women face. Ain't nobody got time for that!

As I closed my laptop, I realized this exchange was a perfect illustration. It's about calling out small, everyday behaviors reinforcing harmful systems. It's about staying committed to pushing back against forces that want to keep us in a tired loop. Yes, everyone remembers Dr. King's "I Have a Dream" speech, but the platform that he stood on was built by every lunch counter sit-in, every person who marched. As we work to swim toward more equitable shores, the sharks—the forces that seek to maintain the status quo—are constantly circling. But that doesn't mean we just let ourselves drown.

Sugarcane Circles

Speaking of circling, we must embrace that our resistance often begins in the quiet, seemingly inconsequential spaces where we learn to imagine something better.

I've referenced my childhood a few times, but I haven't really provided much background. When I was between the ages of four and fifteen, my family lived on Guam, "where America's day begins" and where my mom is originally from. When we first moved to the island, we lived well outside the city limits, surrounded by jungle walls, sharing a compound of houses with aunts, uncles, and cousins. We were poor—dirt poor. Mom and Dad worked long hours, and without screens to occupy us, our afternoons after school were our own.

The days during summer vacations provided a particularly blank canvas, and we spent our time on the beach or exploring the nearby jungle. One such day, while wandering through the trees, my cousins and I stumbled upon a large patch of sugarcane. As kids, this new discovery could only mean one thing—a fort! Armed with nothing but an old two-by-four, some rope, and our boundless imagination, we got to work.

It wasn't easy, but we were determined. Eventually, we created a clearing just large enough for us to sit together. There, in our circle, we shared snacks, told stories, occasionally fought (as siblings and cousins do), and passed the time in ways that felt sacred.

Why am I sharing this story with you?

Looking back, that sugarcane circle wasn't just a place to play. It was a lesson in seeing something that wasn't yet possible, and creating space where none existed before. As importantly, the sugarcane circle reminds us that challenging entrenched systems is *hard*. It takes labor, collective effort, and courage to insist that something new can exist where only the old once thrived. Blisters formed on our hands, tempers flared, and sometimes we wanted to give up. Even when it was complete, we were continually forced to rebuild when storms inevitably tore through. Resistance, like that sugarcane fort, demands perseverance and resolve.

There is one more sugarcane metaphor I'd like to leave you with. As I mentioned, the space was small, with barely enough room for all my siblings and cousins. But one morning, some boys from down the road happened across our little fort while they were en route to their own adventures. They asked if they could play, too.

We could have hung a "No Trespassing" sign. But instead, we invited them in and did the necessary work to widen the circle. My brother's friend once showed up with pizza rolls, so it's not like we were going to keep him out, either. And so it went. As others came to join our merry band, we kept widening the circle to welcome new perspectives. All it required was our willingness.

This is what the system fears most: not loud, rebellious declarations, but the quiet determination of those who refuse to accept its terms. The sugarcane circle wasn't just a fort. It was a reminder that small resistance, even with the simplest tools, creates transformation, and the influence ripples outward. So, ask yourself: What would it take to clear a space for something new—within your world, your workplace, your relationships, or yourself?

Rebel *with* a Cause

Remember the "ladies who lunch"? I think there's one more lesson to extract from my experience with those fancy, big-haired belles of the ball.

I've always had a soft spot for alliteration. Something about the rhythm and melody of words tumbling together fascinates me. But knee-deep in the world of these "ladies," my penchant for playful language took on a more mischievous edge. In a small act of rebellion, I began assigning nicknames to the cruelest culprits in their cohort. I decided that these women, who couldn't be bothered to show us the respect of learning our names, hadn't earned the honor of us using theirs.

Brake Pad Barbie, for example, was so titled for her ties to the automotive industry and her uncanny resemblance to the iconic doll. Moaning Myrtle, for her perpetual complaints (and the one time we caught her in a closet with a "friend"). Hot Pocket Heiress, Bootcamp Becky . . . the list went on, capturing their quirks or the week's latest antics. I wouldn't say I'm proud of it, per se, but after long days, I'd unwind with a glass of wine, a trashy reality show flickering in the background, and jot down new ideas in my burn book. It was my way of decompressing and reclaiming a sense of power in a world where we had so little.

Was it nice? Absolutely not. Did I care? Not in the slightest. The nicknames weren't just an outlet for my frustration—they were a way to cope with years of toxic treatment, of being belittled and brushed aside by women who wielded their wealth like a weapon.

These nicknames caught on quickly and became a kind of shorthand among the staff, a secret language that bonded us together against the absurdity of it all. We vented our frustrations, laughed—and, in a way, they gave us the strength to keep doing the work that actually mattered, even if it was often over-shadowed by the spectacle.

Looking back, though, I've come to realize that other than providing a boost to office morale, this practice did little to serve a greater cause. Let me explain. That private act of rebellion affected no change in our situation, in the lives of those around us, or in the structures that facilitated the inequitable conditions we operated in. So when I talk about not playing "nice," it's important to narrow down my meaning and to share my own evolution in this journey.

I'm reminded of another icon, Rosa Parks, who could not have envisioned the impact that her act of resistance would set in motion. Her rebellion is often credited with being the ripple that turned into a tidal wave, the spark that lit the forest ablaze (choose your metaphor) to awaken so many to the cause and incite momentum for the Civil Rights Movement. But why? I believe it's because when she decided to stop playing nice, to refuse to be relegated to the back of the bus, she stood directly against the tyranny of the status quo and challenged the world-view of what would have been perceived as acceptable.

Her act sparked the Montgomery bus boycott, disrupting systemic racism in public transportation. But the real power came from the organized, sustained effort that followed, culminating in a Supreme Court ruling to end segregation on buses. It wasn't just about dismantling injustice; it was about building a new, more just framework that serves everyone. A world where power is shared, not hoarded. A world where our actions reflect our ideals.

Building such a world demands accountability, imagination, and collaboration. It's unglamorous, messy, and rarely celebrated, but it is where lasting progress takes shape.

Similarly, our resistance must have purpose. If we are going to have nerve, our intention must extend beyond ourselves, our feelings, and even those of our coworkers. It must directly confront the systems that would otherwise operate unchecked and unseen. Maybe you won't be recognized with your own federal holiday in the end, but that doesn't mean the actions you take won't reverberate through history.

PROMISING PRACTICE 9
Curiosity on Purpose

Curiosity—the active pursuit of questions and understanding—allows us to examine our daily interactions and assumptions, acknowledge failures, and refine strategies. Science shows that curiosity

- **Broadens perspective:** Curious people explore multiple viewpoints, which helps them better understand interconnected systems and identify the root causes of problems.

- **Drives problem solving:** Studies in neuroscience reveal that curiosity enhances memory and learning, enabling us to absorb and apply new ideas effectively.

- **Fosters empathy:** Curiosity about others' experiences reduces bias and strengthens relationships, creating conditions for more equitable collaboration.

Here's how we can cultivate curiosity as a practical tool for ensuring that our actions are purposeful in driving change:

1. **Ask "Why?" five times.**

   Toyota developed the *5 Whys* method, which helps uncover root causes by repeatedly asking "Why?" This technique forces us to move beyond superficial

(CONTINUED)

questions and vague answers and interrogate the deeper systems at play. Don't stop at the first "why" and be satisfied with surface-level fixes. Persist, asking uncomfortable questions to uncover hidden truths.

Example:

- Why are certain groups underrepresented in leadership?
- Why aren't their contributions recognized?
- Why do mentorship programs fail to address this gap?
- Why isn't systemic bias acknowledged openly?
- Why aren't policies changing despite awareness?

This process doesn't just highlight flaws; it forces us to revisit assumptions and build strategies that address the root causes.

2. Design for disruption.

Curiosity thrives in environments that challenge norms. Design activities that disrupt the comfortable rhythm of things and invite reflection.

Actionable steps:

- **Conduct "assumption audits."** Regularly examine organizational beliefs, policies, and norms by asking critical questions: What are we assuming? Who benefits? Who is excluded? What if the group typically seen as a problem holds the most untapped potential? What if leadership structures prioritized historically marginalized employees? These shifts expose hidden biases and reveal new strategies.

- **Introduce perspective-shifting scenarios.** Revisit existing narratives and dynamics by flipping roles or perspectives. Retell *Goldilocks* from the bears' perspective: a family protecting their home. Apply this lens to workplace dynamics: Who is the "Goldilocks" disrupting the system? Who are the "bears" resisting exploitation? This practice reveals blind spots and encourages adaptive solutions.

- **Encourage open dialogue.** Facilitate discussions that make space for discomfort and deeper analysis rather than reinforcing the status quo.

- **Prototype small changes.** Experiment with structural adjustments in decision-making, hiring, and leadership, iterating based on feedback. For example, an organization might revisit its hiring practices by piloting blind recruitment in one department. It could then track outcomes, adjust based on feedback, and expand the practice iteratively. Each step refines the approach while ensuring long-term change.

By embedding disruption into organizational practices, teams can uncover hidden biases and adjust their approaches for more equitable and effective outcomes.

3. **Reframe setbacks as opportunities.**

Setbacks are inevitable in transformation, but curiosity treats them as data for improvement.

What to do:

- **Acknowledge and analyze.** When an initiative underperforms, assess what worked, what didn't, and why. For example, if a DEI program sees

(CONTINUED)

low engagement, review participation data to identify gaps.

- **Gather feedback.** Engage employees and stake-holders to understand barriers and uncover ways to improve accessibility, messaging, or execution.

- **Adjust and iterate.** Use insights to refine the approach, test changes, and reintroduce the initiative in a more effective way.

- **Normalize continuous learning.** Foster a culture where setbacks are seen as part of progress, not reasons to abandon meaningful efforts.

By treating challenges as opportunities for growth, organizations can create sustainable, long-term impact.

9

Break the Back Row Barrier

For leaders, the burden doubles—you're accountable for yourself and those you lead. Challenging systems demands awareness of power dynamics to stand in the gap for others. And so, my final story...

Before I left the nonprofit world for agency life, I was an executive at a storied organization with over sixty years of history. The downside of its institutional longevity was a well-entrenched bastion of hierarchy, where titles, tenure, testosterone, and, yes, skin tone often set the standard. But, since I was there, I was determined to shake things up.

Cecilia and Ainsley (*names changed for privacy*) were two of the rising stars on my team. Cecilia was a young Latina with fierce intelligence, ambition, and sharp wit. Ainsley, who was Jewish, was equally driven and brought a wealth of experience and valuable perspective.

For an upcoming board meeting, they had taken the lead on a research project that my team was responsible for, and they had done a phenomenal job. Given that they had done the lion's share of the work and knew the information best, I thought it was only appropriate that they should have the chance to be acknowledged and have a voice in the room. It was a rare opportunity; junior staffers weren't traditionally allowed to present directly to the board, and I was excited for them.

But the morning of the meeting, as I was going over my own talking points, I heard a knock at my office door. Cecilia and Ainsley entered, their expressions a mix of confusion and discomfort.

"Is everything okay?" I asked, gesturing for them to sit.

Ainsley spoke first, her voice steady but tinged with hurt and frustration. "Amira," she began, "we just had an . . . interesting run-in with Jake." Cecilia took a deep breath. "When we arrived in the boardroom for meeting prep, Jake told us we'd have to sit in the back row of the board room." Ainsley nodded. "We asked him why, and he laughed and said we should be grateful to be in the room."

I closed my eyes momentarily, envisioning the large oval table in the boardroom. There were undoubtedly more than enough chairs for everyone. A guttural anger bubbled up inside me, a reminder of all the times I'd seen women, especially women of color, pushed to the back row in rooms where they had earned a seat—of all the times it had happened to me.

"Go grab a cup of coffee," I told them, already on the move. "I'll come get you in a moment."

I found Jake milling about outside the boardroom. He looked smug as he seemed to be practicing his handshake, positioning himself to be the first to greet the board. "Jake," I said, keeping my voice even, "we need to talk about Cecilia and Ainsley."

He looked up, feigning concern. "Oh? Is there an issue?"

"Yes," I replied, my tone calm but direct. I turned around and walked to my office, knowing he'd have to follow. Jake was a senior leader at the organization, but not as senior as me—and I felt like he needed a reminder of that. "Apparently, you told two members of my team to sit in the back row of the room and suggested they should be grateful to be invited. Explain why you thought that was appropriate."

He was clearly caught off guard, but quickly masked it with a smirk. "Oh, that," he chuckled, "they just misinterpreted. I was only joking. Besides, they made a rude comment about how I love giving a grand speech. You know, they basically implied that I was some kind of kiss-ass or something. I was flustered! They threw me off my game."

I crossed my arms, refusing to let him spin this back on them. "They *basically implied*? Do you have any idea what you're *explicitly* telling women when you ask them to be *grateful* for an opportunity they've worked incredibly hard for? And how dismissing them to the back of the room—a room in which they're scheduled to present—diminishes their contributions? Now you're saying *they* made *you* uncomfortable?"

Jake shifted awkwardly in his seat, his confident facade beginning to crack. "Look, Amira, I didn't mean anything by it. I was just—"

I cut him off. "Jake, if you feel flustered by a little bit of banter from two staff members, perhaps you should think about why that is. My team deserves respect, and they'll be sitting at the table, where they belong. This is a professional environment, and it's my expectation that everyone here is treated with the dignity they deserve."

He flushed slightly but didn't offer an apology, instead muttering something about "misunderstandings" and "taking things too personally."

"You can go now. You'll want to be on your game for your speech."

I found Cecilia and Ainsley in their cubicles. Both looked up expectantly.

"Jake won't be a problem," I assured them.

The three of us walked to the boardroom together, and I couldn't help but notice the air of confidence that we all moved with. I also couldn't suppress a small smirk of my own as everyone watched us take our seats.

"Más o Menos"

You see, leaders like Jake operate from a scarcity mindset—fear of losing reputation, revenue, relationships, or relevance. Acting from this place of fear distorts how people think and act. In fact, a study on farmers before harvest, when financial strain is high, revealed diminished performance on cognitive tests. After harvest, when resources were plentiful, their performance improved.[1] This is because the pressure of scarcity absorbs mental bandwidth, leaving less capacity for complex thinking. This same dynamic plays out in many aspects of life.

When we perceive resources—whether time, money, or social capital—as limited, we focus narrowly on immediate needs at the expense of long-term vision. Scarcity thinking results in fear-driven choices, holding us in reactive cycles and preventing us from imagining alternatives or taking bold action.[2] In environments where preservation feels more critical than progress, people hold tightly to what they feel is theirs. This includes shutting out those perceived as threats.

This mindset extends beyond individuals: entire systems thrive on scarcity thinking. Marketing campaigns exploit it with urgency-driven messages like "limited time only." Workplace cultures reward relentless productivity, discouraging rest or reflection.

Even personal relationships can fall victim to scarcity, where fear of losing approval silences honest communication. Much of our current political discourse is framed around this type of thinking. If people are afraid for their jobs, for their values, for their societal standing—for the price of eggs—they will demonize others and even vote against their own interests in an attempt at self-preservation.

Yet scarcity is often more perception than reality. Shifting to an abundance mindset doesn't deny limitations; it reframes them. An abundance mindset reframes risk as opportunity, fostering courage, creativity, and a broader perspective, allowing people to see the potential benefits rather than just the costs. When individuals believe there's enough to go around, it expands their focus, enabling them to prioritize systemic change and future impact over short-term comfort. Crucially, people see others as allies rather than competitors, creating a fertile ground for collective action where people feel supported and empowered to act together.

The real danger of scarcity isn't just missed opportunities—it's the loss of potential. Moving beyond scarcity thinking and leading from an abundance mindset allows us to act purposefully, not because the risks disappear but because we recognize the value of what we are fighting for. When we stop framing decisions through the lens of what we lack, we gain the clarity to see what we stand to lose.

Not Doing Nothing

Speaking of loss of potential...

As the saying goes, "The secret of getting ahead is getting started." As we close out the "Do" portion of the book, there is one point that I can't possibly emphasize enough:

The concept of inevitability is a trap we cannot afford to get stuck in.

This mindset—consciously or unconsciously held—rests on the idea that no matter what we do or fail to do, the world will inevitably become better, fairer, and more just. It is so deeply entrenched in many of us that we abandon accountability and lull ourselves into the belief that good, *somehow*, prevails. This myth keeps us in a comfort-induced paralysis, willfully ignorant of the world's evils. We convince ourselves that if we wait long enough and keep our heads down, justice and equality will manifest on their own.

Decades ago, Martin Luther King Jr. aptly stated, "The arc of the moral universe is long but it bends toward justice."[3] Those who interpret this as an endorsement of inevitability entirely miss the point of his exhortation. I believe—and the nature of Dr. King's life, and death, affirms—that *it does not bend without our intentional action.* Every civil rights victory, every labor reform, every step toward gender equality or social justice was achieved through deliberate, relentless action.[4] The scales of justice don't self-correct; they remain weighted by oppression and the inertia of the status quo.

Believing in inevitability allows us to claim we're on "the right side of history" without doing the work to earn that position. But rights can be rolled back, and freedoms eroded. For every hard-won gain, forces exist that will claw it back if we're not vigilant and proactive. The belief that "we've come too far to go back" has repeatedly been shattered.

Imagine if the suffragettes had waited for voting rights to manifest. If civil rights leaders had stayed silent, hoping segregation would dissolve. If LGBTQIA+ advocates trusted equality to emerge without relentless advocacy. Progress is never the result of passive optimism. It's the product of deliberate, sustained disruption.

The world evolves through solidarity, action, and an unwavering refusal to accept what is. The idea that justice will "just happen" is a dangerous delusion. The future we want is ours to build.

"Deny, Defend, Depose"

When systems are left unchallenged and injustices allowed to fester, the illusion of inevitability collides with growing frustration in those systems. The tragic events of December 2024 serve as a sobering example of what unfolds when a broken system reaches that breaking point.

In the cold twilight of a bustling New York City street, the city's usual din was pierced by the chilling finality of gunfire, and UnitedHealthcare CEO Brian Thompson's body lay sprawled on the concrete.

The news triggered a wave of reactions ranging from shock and unease to grim satisfaction and even outright celebration, a stark reminder of mounting resentment toward corporate power. On social media, influencers and their followers expressed a striking lack of sympathy. Others called it a harbinger of accountability, a warning shot for the entire health insurance industry.[5] The reaction was not just about one man's death—it was an indictment of a system that, for too long, had ignored the suffering of the people it was supposed to serve.

As the investigation progressed, a chilling detail gripped the public's attention. The bullet casings left at the scene bore three meticulously etched words: Deny, Defend, Depose. These three words were more than a cryptic message to a slain CEO. They echoed a well-known critique popularized in the 2010 exposé *Delay, Deny, Defend: Why Insurance Companies Don't Pay Claims and What You Can Do About It*.[6] The book had laid bare a system that, for decades, had profited from exploiting the vulnerable, and Thompson had been one of its highest gatekeepers.

Let me be one million percent crystal clear: *I am in no way implying, inferring, or in any uncertain terms condoning this act of violence.* Too often, transformation has been born from violence and has shaped history—from the founding of this country to the end of enslavement. But transformation rooted in fear or domination rarely leads to justice. The kind worth pursuing must be built on dignity, courage, and shared humanity.

The only reason I bring it up is this: When met with public backlash following the most violent possible act of aggression, the response of these corporations was ... *to take pictures off their websites.* In a desperate act of self-preservation, several major insurance and healthcare companies began scrubbing their web pages of executive biographies. Senior leaders vanished from public view, hiding behind anonymity and corporate walls. Security firms were brought in. The public wondered in one voice: "Why protect your CEOs when you should protect your customers?"

It was as if the industry was taunting the public, doubling down on the practices that fueled resentment. In fact, the day after Thompson's assassination, BlueCross BlueShield announced a controversial new policy: Anesthesia coverage would be denied for surgeries exceeding a specific, arbitrary timeline. Outrage was immediate and fierce. I mean, I'm sure the announcement had been scheduled well in advance, but ... read the room! We also learned that State Farm had removed fire protection from many of its policyholders,[7] as we watched 100 mph wind-fueled wildfires rip across Los Angeles, destroying homes and shattering lives.

Inevitability Is a Lie

Actual change comes from collective action, solidarity, and an unwavering commitment to justice. Systems don't reform themselves; in fact, they will dig in to resist reform. Certainly, there is a larger conversation to be had about capitalism and the American "healthcare" system. But progress will only be won with relentless advocacy and the courage to confront entrenched power.

Days after their controversial announcement, BlueCross BlueShield reversed course and reinstated full anesthesia coverage.[8] The retreat was a symbolic victory, a rare acknowledgment that public outrage, when people refuse to be silenced, sidelined, or ignored, becomes an unstoppable force for change.

PROMISING PRACTICE 10
A Fitness Exam

Leadership requires more than technical skills; it demands capacities to navigate a dynamic, unpredictable world. Leaders who can identify their own strengths and growth opportunities are better equipped to recognize and nurture them in others.

The Harvard Leadership Fitness framework equips individuals to confront complexity and lead with courage and conviction. It focuses on four key dimensions that help leaders interpret challenges, adapt, and act purposefully:[9]

1. **Balance:** The capacity to navigate paradoxes and tensions without rushing to simplistic solutions.

   - **Why it matters:** Nice leaders often prioritize maintaining peace, avoiding discomfort, or making quick decisions to quell tension. Leaders with balance embrace complexity, holding space for multiple truths and contradictions.

   - **Actionable step:** In difficult conversations, resist the urge to resolve tension immediately. Instead,

(CONTINUED)

use both/and thinking to recognize the validity
of differing perspectives and guide teams toward
solutions that honor complexity.

2. **Strength:** The ability to recognize and cultivate unique
talents in oneself and others and leverage those
strengths for impact.

  - **Why it matters:** Nice leaders may avoid acknowl-
    edging their own gaps or fail to harness the
    strengths of diverse teams, which limits growth.
    Strong leaders invest in their own development
    and actively elevate others.

  - **Actionable step:** Take a strengths-based approach
    in team development. Identify individual strengths,
    align tasks to maximize impact, and model vulner-
    ability by openly acknowledging areas where you
    rely on others to complement your skills.

3. **Flexibility:** The willingness to adapt strategies and
approaches in response to evolving circumstances or
needs.

  - **Why it matters:** Nice leaders may use famil-
    iar methods to avoid discomfort or disruption.
    Flexible leaders challenge their biases, embrace
    change, and experiment with new ways of thinking
    and acting.

  - **Actionable step:** Reflect on a recent challenge
    and ask yourself: What assumptions might I need
    to question? Seek feedback from a diverse group
    of peers and incorporate new perspectives into
    your approach.

4. **Endurance:** The capacity to persevere through setbacks and challenges while focusing on long-term goals.

- **Why it matters:** Nice leaders may prioritize short-term wins or shy away from challenge to avoid discomfort, but enduring leaders remain purposeful, even during adversity.

- **Actionable step:** During moments of difficulty, reconnect with your broader purpose. Reframe challenges as steps in a larger journey, and intentionally carve out time for recovery and reflection to sustain your energy and focus.

For leaders committed to meaningful change, looking to dismantle the "back row barrier" and ensure that power is equitably distributed, these four leadership capacities are critical. These dimensions are not just tools—they are essential practices for thriving in today's demanding environment.

PROMISING PRACTICE 11
Be Perfectly Assertive

Perfectly assertive communication—a balanced approach of being neither overly aggressive nor passive—empowers leaders to confront systemic behaviors, especially when those situations involve power dynamics or implicit bias.[10]

These behaviors will help you to be perfectly assertive in your communication as you bridge the gap between

(CONTINUED)

"nice" (avoiding confrontation) and "nerve" (disrupting the status quo), reinforcing a culture of equity and respect.

- **Observation with empathy:** Never sidestep an issue or dilute its significance by framing it as a mere misunderstanding. Address the matter promptly and assertively, while providing an opportunity for differing perspectives to be shared.

- **Fostering dialogue and accountability:** Refuse to let excuses or deflections derail the conversation. This practice balances respect for the individual with clear accountability for their actions.

- **Clear and purposeful action:** Identify the issue, but also set clear expectations for change. This ensures the focus remains on the behavior and its impact rather than personal defensiveness.

- **Following through:** Assertive communication isn't just about confronting the issue—it's also about empowering those affected to move forward with confidence.

PART IV
REVISIT

10

The Circle of Life

W e've come to the final part of our four-part framework: Revisit. Progress along the Nice to Nerve Continuum is not a straight line; it's a circle. Change is not a one-time event but a continuous process of learning and adaptation.

At its core, revisiting hinges on the distinction between a fixed mindset and a growth mindset, shaping how individuals and systems approach change, setbacks, and progress:

- A *fixed mindset* believes character, intelligence, and abilities are static and tends to focus on goals viewed as easily achievable, avoiding failure to preserve a fragile sense of worth. This mindset clings to the existing order, prioritizing comfort over growth and evading the discomfort required for transformation.

- A *growth mindset* thrives on challenges, prioritizing curiosity and viewing failure as a chance to stretch and improve. Setbacks provide valuable data for future action; success reflects effort and resilience.

Apathy and complacency are constant threats, tempting us to believe the work is done or that it doesn't matter. Revisiting is the antidote to stagnation, keeping us engaged and ensuring we continue to hold ourselves and others accountable. Revisiting embraces the impermanence of transformation, urging us to constantly iterate and refine strategies. It means facing discomfort and rethinking what we thought we knew. Growth demands it.

Revisiting is a tool for reclaiming the nerve that has been socialized out of us. Revisit your assumptions. Revisit your narratives. Revisit your heroes and villains. Rethink your values and reimagine a more equitable world. Question every system and every actor within those systems, including yourself.

By revisiting with intention, we ensure the pursuit of change evolves alongside the complexities of our systems and the challenges we face. Revisiting sharpens resistance into sustained progress. Justice and transformation aren't destinations; they're ongoing journeys that require consistent participation. Revisiting is a commitment to show up again and again—not perfectly, but purposefully.

I would like to stress that Part IV is not short on significance, though it is by far the shortest in length. It's only this one chapter—and it's not even a long one. I'm not really introducing much in the way of new information here, and the beauty of it is, I don't need to repeat any concepts—just *revisit* the rest of the book! Feel free to underline, highlight, or use Post-it Tabs as needed.

As we come to a close, I wondered what the best way to wrap things up would be. And then I figured, let's play a game!

Ready, Player 1

Have you ever played Red Rover? Maybe at school? *Ah, memories* . . . grass-stained jeans, laughter, and the risk of serious injury. A little while ago, it occurred to me that the game, in many ways, mimicked the way systems operate. Picture it in your mind's eye . . .

For those unfamiliar with Red Rover, or in need of a refresher, here are the basics:

1. Two teams form parallel lines, facing each other, joining hands to create a human chain.

2. Each team takes turns calling out: "Red Rover, Red Rover, send [insert name] right over!"

3. The named player runs at full speed toward the opposing team, attempting to break through their chain.

4. If they succeed, they claim a player from the opposing team to join theirs; if they fail, they join the opposition.

5. The game continues until one team has absorbed all the players (or until recess is over!).

In this metaphor, one team represents systemic barriers—norms, policies, and power structures designed to resist change—with those willing to challenge them lined up on the other side. When attacks come, will we stand firm in our resolve? How will you respond when you meet opposition? The reason I've included this in the "Revisit" section is a phenomenon I call the *Red Rover Recoil*: The exhaustion and frustration of repeatedly confronting barriers tests one's resolve against forces like complacency and performative allyship.

Initially, you stand firm, calling for change. But when the other team comes charging back at you, are you prepared to endure the pain? Or will you let go? Meanwhile, others who were adamant about their willingness to learn and "do better" may falter when they meet resistance. Maybe not the first time, but the pressure of having to run at the wall again and again may break them down to the point that they even assimilate willingly.

Progress is always hard-won. Revisiting strengthens your stance and ensures you hold the line, even when it feels easier to let go. This is your invitation to "Come on over!"

In the end, the call is simple: think critically, feel deeply, do consistently, and revisit frequently. True change begins within—and when you transform yourself, you create the foundation to transform the world.

This brings us to our final Promising Practice. The key to change isn't just strength—it's strategy. And strategy requires revisiting the rules, questioning who benefits, and designing systems that foster equity rather than exclusion.

PROMISING PRACTICE 12
Don't Hate the Player, Hate the Game

Games are microcosms of systems, with rules that shape who wins, who loses, and how power is distributed. They allow us to explore systems thinking.[1] And just like the games, systems don't change unless we adopt an infinite mindset in order to collaboratively revisit their rules, rethink their dynamics, and challenge the structures that keep them in place.[2]

Systems thinking is about seeing the big picture—recognizing how roles and relationships create outcomes. In applying this lens to the game of Red Rover, we might ask:

- Why do some players succeed while others fail?

- How does the chain maintain its strength, and what makes it vulnerable?

- What changes could make the game fairer or more inclusive?

Systems thinking isn't just about finding patterns or fixing problems—it's about understanding how ideas flow, how people interact, and how change happens. Communication is at the heart of every system. Whether working as a team, making decisions, or challenging the status quo, communication drives outcomes.

The game of Red Rover provides a hands-on way to explore these ideas by showing how rules and communication create systems that either help people or hold them back. By redesigning the game, participants can better understand how to challenge and improve the systems they interact with daily.

Steps to Redesign the Game

Step 1: Imagine the rules

Picture the original rules of Red Rover. Teams link arms, and players try breaking the chain. Consider:

- What do these rules reveal about the system?

- Who has an advantage, and who is left struggling?

Step 2: Play the mental game

Imagine playing the game under these original rules. Pay attention to patterns:

- Who breaks through the chain most often?

- What strategies work best?

(CONTINUED)

Step 3: Change the rules

Now, imagine redesigning the rules to make the game more equitable. For example:

- Rotate player positions after every turn to balance strong and weak links.
- Allow players to pair up to reinforce vulnerable spots in the chain.

Step 4: Play the new game

Visualize playing the redesigned game. Consider:

- How do the changes affect the system?
- Does it feel more balanced or collaborative?
- What new strategies emerge?

Step 5: Reflect on the changes

How did the new rules shift power and communication? Ask yourself:

- Did the changes make the game fairer?
- How did new communication patterns—like collaboration or inclusive decision-making—impact the system?

Think of this exercise as a workout for your mind. There's less of a chance you'll dislocate your shoulder that way. The principles outlined next will help you strengthen your ability to see how systems operate and identify opportunities for change. The more you practice, the more heightened your systems thinking skills will become. Over time, you'll retrain your mind to intuitively recognize similar patterns and rules in everyday life—at home, at work, in relationships, and within larger institutions.

Six Principles of Systems Thinking and Communication

1. **Everything's connected**

   - **Systems thinking:** Every link in the chain matters. Similarly, in real-world systems, every decision and action is interconnected.

   - **Communication:** How teams strategize and share ideas shapes outcomes. Better communication strengthens the chain—or the system.

2. **What's under the surface?**

   - **Systems thinking:** Visible struggles—like breaking through the chain—often mask deeper issues, like imbalanced rules or hidden biases.

   - **Communication:** Barriers in how we talk or listen can reinforce these deeper problems.

3. **Combining pieces**

   - **Systems thinking:** Combining resources and perspectives leads to innovation. Pairing players strengthens weak links.

   - **Communication:** Collaboration and sharing ideas ensure every voice contributes to the solution.

4. **Feedback loops**

   - **Systems thinking:** Repeated failures cause discouragement, while success builds momentum. Changing rules can create positive feedback loops so all players stay engaged.

   - **Communication:** Honest feedback and open dialogue build trust, reinforcing positive cycles.

(CONTINUED)

5. **Cause and effect**
   - **Systems thinking:** Small rule changes can ripple through the system, creating significant effects.
   - **Communication:** Simple adjustments in communication can transform outcomes.

6. **Seeing the big picture**
   - **Systems thinking:** The game isn't just about individual moves—it's about how the whole system works together.
   - **Communication:** Every conversation and strategy shapes the larger system. Understanding this helps us build stronger connections.

The Lesson: Shaking the System

Whether you imagine Red Rover or another game entirely, this exercise reveals how systems are designed to maintain power—and how they can be redesigned for equity. Niceness keeps the chain tightly linked, resisting change. Nerve challenges the chain, pushing for progress. Using systems thinking helps us understand how to break through, redesign the rules, and transform the system.

Rethink the game, rebuild the system. When you're running toward the chain, remember that true transformation doesn't just change the players—it changes the game itself. But transformation is not permanent, and the game doesn't play itself. If you don't actively challenge the rules and stay engaged, progress falters, and hard-won changes risk being undone by the illusion of inevitability.

As you reflect on the lessons of this book, ask yourself: What systems have you silently upheld because comfort felt safer or easier than confrontation? What's the first rule you need to challenge? What's one change you can make today? This isn't just about dismantling external systems; it's about rethinking the internal ones, too.

CONCLUSION

Cost Analysis

I teach my daughter a simple lesson: Leave people and places better than you found them.

The work begins here. I hope that, by now, I don't have to convince you that comfort isn't sustainable. Progress demands rejecting the compulsion of comfort in favor of community and collective courage.

The compulsion of comfort isn't easy to overcome, but by recognizing and naming it, we take steps toward building a world that works for all of us. This is solidarity: working together across differences to demand that systems serve everyone, not just a privileged few. By embracing discomfort, we increase our capacity for growth, transformation, and renewal. And yet, so many of us remain tethered to comfort because it feels safer than the alternative.

My purpose in writing this book is not to shame you for the impact "nice" has on your life. That's like blaming sexual assault on a short skirt—it shifts accountability away from the perpetrators. On the contrary, this is a call for acknowledgment and collective action. It's about holding those in power accountable while also demanding that we start with the person in the mirror. Institutions are made of individuals. The system crumbles a little more with every person who moves from slumber to woke, from awake to doing the work—as it should. We are not powerless. And that's precisely why they want us to play nice.

This book memorializes how I move through the world. That doesn't mean things will look exactly the same for you (nor should they!). Remember, this book is not a blueprint, it's a tool kit. But I would be remiss, maybe irresponsible—even unethical— if I didn't also help you understand the conditions in which we challenge these systems. *Now, the decision is yours: Will you pay the price of nerve, or continue shouldering the cost of nice?*

Make no mistake, there is a cost to choosing nerve over nice.

I can sense your eyes rolling. *"Oh, sure. Now she tells us!"*

For you to comprehend the price of nerve, I had to establish that the cost of remaining nice is one we can't afford. If I'd told you about that price up front, without showing you the harm, you might have run before Chapter 1.

Bottom line: External pressure will not collapse systems. They crumble when the people within question the constructs on which they're built.

To step into the antihero role, we must refuse to accept things as they are. This spark ignites transformation and signals the beginning of the end for the status quo. That's when things get messy. When people recognize they deserve better, the scaffolding supporting oppression begins to sway, and the facade cracks. For all its supposed strength, it's a straw house, after all.

This is the not-so-secret secret: Systems that demand compliance are sustained by our complicity.[1] That's why we are witnessing the unsettling regression of progress that once felt inevitable. After a period where some even claimed we had moved into a "post-racial" America, the system counted on us being easily appeased, more eager for comfort than committed to change. The system thought it could placate us by painting "Black Lives Matter" on a few streets while injustices went unchecked.

Meanwhile, the proverbial "they"—those who benefit from maintaining the status quo—desperately want us to avoid saying the quiet parts aloud. They fear what happens when we decide that "good enough" is no longer a sufficient response to our condition.

And yet, in our righteous indignation, we must also reckon with the cost of defiance—to reputation, relationships, even livelihood. But more dangerous than speaking the truth is not speaking at all. History shows that empires are not toppled by well-wishers; they are dismantled by the unyielding resolve of those who refuse to comply in the face of oppression.

Paying the Cost

As my friend La Vida Johnson says, "I've never seen anyone sell their soul to the devil and get some change back!" It's a one-sided exchange. I promised not to sugarcoat anything, and I won't start now. They killed Martin. They killed Malcolm. They killed Fred Hampton. Hell, they killed JFK and Abraham Lincoln too. And they burned Tulsa to the ground. The cost of truth-telling is high; it may not take your life, but that doesn't mean the price won't be extracted in other ways. Yet, the impact of such bravery ripples far beyond the moment, paving the way for justice and systemic change.

At fifteen years old, Malala Yousafzai was shot in the head by the Taliban for advocating girls' education in Pakistan. Despite life-threatening injuries and immense trauma, she refused to retreat, amplifying her voice on the global stage and becoming the youngest-ever Nobel Peace Prize laureate. Malala's journey reveals the profound personal risk incurred when defying oppressive systems and the unyielding commitment required to push forward.

Nelson Mandela endured twenty-seven years of imprisonment for his fight to end apartheid in South Africa. Despite the physical and psychological toll, he emerged resolutely, leading his nation toward equality. Mandela's life is a testament to the patience, perseverance, and strength needed to achieve systemic change.

Actual change demands this kind of unwavering commitment. Yet, even in the darkest moments, there is purpose: the understanding that today's discomfort is the price of tomorrow's liberation.

Consider Dr. Christine Blasey Ford's testimony against Supreme Court nominee Brett Kavanaugh in 2018. Standing up for truth and accountability, she faced public scrutiny, harassment, and death threats, forcing her to move homes. Her courage exposed the societal cost of holding powerful men accountable and the isolation that often follows doing the right thing.

Anita Hill paid a similar price in 1991 when she testified against Supreme Court nominee Clarence Thomas, accusing him of sexual harassment. Hill endured public ridicule and was branded a liar, yet her bravery reshaped national conversations on workplace harassment, inspiring future generations to speak out despite the personal toll.

Stepping into the antihero role often strains relationships. Friends and colleagues, even family members who once stood beside you may retreat. This path tests even the most steadfast resolve. The cost is paid in sleepless nights, repeated battles, and the weight of knowing that doing what's right doesn't often bring immediate reward.

Marsha P. Johnson, a Black transgender activist and pivotal figure in the 1969 Stonewall uprising, faced constant harassment, job insecurity, and housing instability amidst her activism. Despite these sacrifices, her relentless fight for justice laid the foundation for the modern LGBTQIA+ rights movement.

Labels like "difficult," "divisive," or "unprofessional" are used to delegitimize dissent and isolate those who push for change, causing reputational harm. This tactic isn't new. The threat of losing one's position, income, or stability isn't a theoretical risk—it's a harsh reality. The entities in place will not go quietly.

Dr. Bennet Omalu, a Nigerian-American forensic neuropathologist, threatened the NFL's interests with his research into chronic traumatic encephalopathy (CTE) in football players. The backlash was swift, isolating him professionally and ending his career in football-related pathology. Yet, his commitment to truth led to critical reforms in player safety and health awareness, proving that the cost of integrity can drive transformative change.

These stories underscore a stark truth: No one escapes the system unscathed. You must choose. Transformative change begins with those willing to take risks. You will not walk this path alone. You stand on the shoulders of those before you—and with those beside you.

The cost is high, but the reward is of far greater worth.

The legacies left behind—the movements sparked and the systemic shifts achieved—prove that sacrifices such as the ones described here pave the way for progress. And despite the risk, the alternative is far more perilous.

Nice? It keeps us compliant, comfortable, and complicit in the systems that harm us.

The stakes of our compliance are not just stagnation—they're erosion. Erosion of our dignity. Erosion of our humanity. Every time we choose palatability over principle, we pay a quiet tax: a little less truth, a little less justice, a little less of ourselves. It means accepting a world that demands our silence and suffering in exchange for crumbs from the table of the powerful and privileged.

This isn't about one moment of courage. It's about committing to a lifetime of resistance, one choice at a time. You cannot change everything, but you *can* change something. And that is enough—so long as you keep going.

Leave people and places better than you found them.

The question we must ask ourselves daily isn't whether we can afford to challenge the carefully constructed social order imposed on us—the real question is, *can we afford not to?*

The price of nice is comfort at the cost of progress. The price of nerve is discomfort in the pursuit of something greater.

I dare you to have the nerve.

NOTES

Preface

1 Charles Duhigg, "The Science Behind Dramatically Better Conversations," TEDx video, filmed September 12, 2024, 12:57, https://www.youtube.com/watch?v=lg48Bi9DA54.

2 Greg Botelho, "What Happened the Night Trayvon Martin Died," *CNN*, May 23, 2012, https://www.cnn.com/2012/05/18/justice/florida-teen-shooting-details/index.html.

3 This quote is widely attributed to Zora Neale Hurston, although no definitive source in her published works has been identified.

4 James R. Detert and Amy C. Edmondson, "Implicit Voice Theories: Taken-for-Granted Rules of Self-Censorship at Work," *Academy of Management Journal* 54, no. 3 (2011): 461–488, https://doi.org/10.5465/amj.2011.61967925.

Introduction

1 Michael H. Kernis and Brian M. Goldman, "A Multicomponent Conceptualization of Authenticity: Theory and Research," *Advances in Experimental Social Psychology* 38 (2006): 283–357, http://dx.doi.org/10.1016/S0065-2601(06)38006-9.

2 M. H. Kuhn, "LEWIN, KURT. *Field Theory of Social Science: Selected Theoretical Papers*. (Edited by Dorwin Cartwright.) Pp. xx, 346. Harper & Brothers, 1951," *The Annals of the American Academy of Political and Social Science* 276, no. 1 (1951): 146–147, https://doi.org/10.1177/000271625127600135.

3 J. O. Prochaska and C. C. DiClemente, "Stages and Processes of Self-Change of Smoking: Toward an Integrative Model of Change,"

Journal of Consulting and Clinical Psychology 51, no. 3 (1983): 390–395, https://doi.org/10.1037/0022-006X.51.3.390.

4   Amy C. Edmondson, *The Fearless Organization: Creating Psychological Safety in the Workplace for Learning, Innovation, and Growth* (John Wiley & Sons, 2018).

5   Jordan Turner, "Employees Seek Personal Value and Purpose at Work. Be Prepared to Deliver," *Gartner*, March 29, 2023, https://www.gartner.com/en/articles/employees-seek-personal-value-and-purpose-at-work-be-prepared-to-deliver.

6   This quote is widely attributed to Maya Angelou, though its exact origin is unknown.

7   John Romano, "James Baldwin: Writing and Talking," *The New York Times*, September 23, 1979, https://www.nytimes.com/1979/09/23/archives/james-baldwin-writing-and-talking-baldwin-baldwin-authors-query.html.

Chapter 1

1   Peter L. Berger and Thomas Luckmann, *The Social Construction of Reality: A Treatise in the Sociology of Knowledge* (Anchor Books, 1967).

2   Merriam-Webster, s.v. "Nice," accessed January 26, 2025, https://www.merriam-webster.com/dictionary/nice.

3   Merriam-Webster, s.v. "Nerve," accessed January 26, 2025, https://www.merriam-webster.com/dictionary/nerve.

4   History.com Editors, "Bikini Introduced," *History*, accessed January 26, 2025, https://www.history.com/this-day-in-history/bikini-introduced.

5   Cathy Malchiodi, "The Body Holds the Healing," *Psychology Today*, December 29, 2022, https://www.psychologytoday.com/us/blog/arts-and-health/202212/the-body-holds-the-healing.

6   Leon A. Jakobovits, "Semantic Satiation and Cognitive Dynamics," *Journal of Special Education* 2, no. 1 (1967): 31–41, https://doi.org/10.1177/002246696700200103.

7   Jodi Summers Holtrop et al., "The Importance of Mental Models in Implementation Science," *Frontiers in Public Health* 9 (2021), https://doi.org/10.3389/fpubh.2021.680316.

8   Adrian Furnham and Hua Chu Boo, "A Literature Review of the Anchoring Effect," *The Journal of Socio-Economics* 40, no. 1 (2011): 35–42, https://doi.org/10.1016/j.socec.2010.10.008.

9   Toni Cade Bambara, "The Education of a Storyteller," in *Deep Sightings and Rescue Missions: Fiction, Essays, and Conversations* (Vintage, 1996), 246–247.

10 The Decision Lab, "Why Do Some Ideas Prompt Other Ideas Later on without Our Conscious Awareness?" *The Decision Lab*, accessed January 27, 2025, https://thedecisionlab.com/biases/priming.

11 The Decision Lab, "Why Do Our Decisions Depend on How Options Are Presented to Us?" *The Decision Lab*, accessed January 27, 2025, https://thedecisionlab.com/biases/framing-effect.

12 Juan Carlos Guerrero, "TIMELINE: Colin Kaepernick's Journey from San Francisco 49ers Star to Kneeling to Protest Racial Injustice," ABC7 News, August 29, 2020, https://abc7news.com/colin-kaepernick-kneeling-when-did-first-kneel-date-what-does-do-now/4147237/.

13 The Decision Lab, "Product Positioning," *The Decision Lab*, accessed January 27, 2025, https://thedecisionlab.com/reference-guide/economics/product-positioning.

14 Hannah Dailey and Kirsten Spruch, "Taylor Swift & Scooter Braun's Feud: A Timeline," *Billboard*, October 25, 2024, https://www.billboard.com/lists/taylor-swift-scooter-braun-feud-timeline/.

15 Mari Matsuda, *Harris Lecture: Mari Matsuda*, YouTube video, 1:07:16, posted by IU Maurer, October 18, 2013, https://www.youtube.com/watch?v=9CjuTLdcLlM.

16 Malcolm X, speech, May 22, 1962, available at Global Research, https://www.globalresearch.ca/malcolm-x-race-crime-police-brutality-you-cant-negro-america-not-have-criminal-record/5716603.

17 Nicholas Epley, *Mindwise: Why We Misunderstand What Others Think, Believe, Feel, and Want* (Vintage Books, 2015).

Chapter 2

1   Ken Robinson, "Do Schools Kill Creativity?" TED video, filmed February 2006, 19:11, https://www.ted.com/talks/sir_ken_robinson_do_schools_kill_creativity.

2   Carrie Tirado Bramen, *American Niceness: A Cultural History* (Harvard University Press, 2017).

3   Erin Blakemore, "Jim Crow Laws Created a Slavery by Another Name," *National Geographic*, February 5, 2020, https://www.nationalgeographic.com/history/article/jim-crow-laws-created-slavery-another-name.

4   See, for example, Luigi Leone and Antonio Chirumbolo, "Conservatism as Motivated Avoidance of Affect: Need for Affect Scales

Predict Conservatism Measures," *Journal of Research in Personality* 42, no. 3 (2007): 755–762, https://doi.org/10.1016/j.jrp.2007.08.001; Alain Van Hiel et al., "The Relationship between Emotional Abilities and Right-Wing and Prejudiced Attitudes," *Emotion* 19, no. 5 (2019): 917–922, https://doi.org/10.1037/emo0000497; and Scott Eidelman et al., "Low-Effort Thought Promotes Political Conservatism," *Personality and Social Psychology Bulletin* 38, no. 6 (2012): 808–820, https://doi .org/10.1177/0146167212439213.

5   David Hagmann, Julia A. Minson, and Catherine H. Tinsley, "Personal Narratives Build Trust across Ideological Divides," *Journal of Applied Psychology* 109, no. 11 (2024): 1693–1715, https://doi.org/10.1037 /apl0001201.

6   Emory Elliott, "The Legacy of Puritanism," Divining America, Teach-erServe©, *National Humanities Center*, accessed January 27, 2025, https://nationalhumanitiescenter.org/tserve/eighteen/ekeyinfo /legacy.htm.

7   History.com Editors, "Roger Williams," *History*, accessed January 27, 2025, https://www.history.com/topics/colonial-america/roger-williams.

8   Robert P. Baird, "The Invention of Whiteness: The Long History of a Dangerous Idea," *The Guardian*, April 20, 2021, https://www .theguardian.com/news/2021/apr/20/the-invention-of-whiteness -long-history-dangerous-idea.

9   Max Weber, *The Protestant Ethic and the Spirit of Capitalism*, trans. Stephen Kalberg (Penguin Classics, 2002).

10 Maria-Letizia Freiin von Bibra, "Manifest Mythmaking: The Role of US 'Manifest Destiny' in Nineteenth and Twenty-First Century Indigenous Dispossession," *The Webster Review of International History* 2, no. 2 (2022): 15–31, https://websterreview.lse.ac.uk/articles/40.

11 Smithsonian Institution, "America's Manifest Destiny," *American Experience*, accessed January 27, 2025, https://americanexperience .si.edu/historical-eras/expansion/pair-westward-apotheosis/.

12 Chimamanda Ngozi Adichie, "The Danger of a Single Story," TED video, filmed July 2009, https://www.ted.com/talks/chimamanda _ngozi_adichie_the_danger_of_a_single_story.

13 Library of Congress, "The Post-War United States, 1945–1968: Overview," Classroom Materials at the Library of Congress, accessed January 27, 2025, https://www.loc.gov/classroom-materials/united-states -history-primary-source-timeline/post-war-united-states-1945-1968 /overview/.

14 See the Jim Crow Museum's collection of scholarly essays at https://
jimcrowmuseum.ferris.edu/links/essays/index.htm.

15 Suzanne Mettler, "How the GI Bill Built the Middle Class and
Enhanced Democracy," *Scholars Strategy Network*, January 1, 2012,
https://scholars.org/contribution/how-gi-bill-built-middle-class
-and-enhanced.

16 Robert Levinson, "Many Black World War II Veterans Were Denied
Their GI Bill Benefits. Time to Fix That," *War on the Rocks*, September
11, 2020. https://warontherocks.com/2020/09/many-black-world
-war-ii-veterans-were-denied-their-gi-bill-benefits-time-to-fix-that/.

17 Suzanne Mettler, "'The Only Good Thing Was the G.I. Bill': Effects of
the Education and Training Provisions on African-American Veterans'
Political Participation," *Studies in American Political Development* 19,
no. 1 (2005): 31–52, https://doi.org/10.1017/S0898588X05000027.

18 Ysolt Usigan, "12 Crazy Vintage Household Ads," *CBS News*, June 3,
2011, https://www.cbsnews.com/pictures/12-crazy-vintage-household
-ads/4/.

19 Evelyn Sommers, *Tyranny of Niceness: Unmasking the Need for
Approval* (Dundurn Press, 2005).

20 Kenna Howat, "Pedaling the Path to Freedom: American Women on
Bicycles," National Women's History Museum, June 27, 2017, https://
www.womenshistory.org/articles/pedaling-path-freedom; Adrienne
LaFrance, "How the Bicycle Paved the Way for Women's Rights," *The
Atlantic*, June 26, 2014, https://www.theatlantic.com/technology
/archive/2014/06/the-technology-craze-of-the-1890s-that-forever
-changed-womens-rights/373535/.

21 History.com Editors, "How World War II Empowered Women," *History*, accessed January 27, 2025, https://www.history.com/news/how
-world-war-ii-empowered-women; Melissa A. McEuen,
"Women, Gender, and World War II," *Oxford Research Encyclopedia
of American History*, June 9, 2016, https://doi.org/10.1093/acrefore
/9780199329175.013.55.

22 Greer Litton Fox, "'Nice Girl': Social Control of Women through a
Value Construct," *Signs* 2, no. 4 (1977): 805–817, http://www.jstor.org
/stable/3173211.

23 Nancy C. Lutkehaus, *Margaret Mead: The Making of an American
Icon* (Princeton University Press, 2008), 261.

24 Hannah Natanson, "Objection to Sexual, LGBTQ Content Propels
Spike in Book Challenges," *The Washington Post*, June 9, 2023,

https://www.washingtonpost.com/education/2023/05/23/lgbtq-book
-ban-challengers/.

25 Resmaa Menakem, *My Grandmother's Hands: Racialized Trauma and the Pathway to Mending Our Hearts and Bodies* (Central Recovery Press, 2017).

Chapter 3

1 Brené Brown, *The Gifts of Imperfection: Let Go of Who You Think You're Supposed to Be and Embrace Who You Are* (Hazelden Publishing, 2010).

2 *The Mind, Explained*, season 2, episode 5, "Brainwashing," aired November 19, 2021, on Netflix, https://www.imdb.com/title/tt15978220/.

3 Emily Feldman and Malia Politzer, "Inside the Dangerous Mission to Understand What Makes Extremists Tick—and How to Change Their Minds," *Time*, September 2, 2020, https://time.com/5881567/extremism
-violence-causes-research/.

4 Nafees Hamid et al., "Neuroimaging 'Will to Fight' for Sacred Values: An Empirical Case Study with Supporters of an Al Qaeda Associate," *Royal Society Open Science* 6, no. 6 (2019): 181585, https://doi.org
/10.1098/rsos.181585.

5 Saul McLeod, "Maslow's Hierarchy of Needs," *Simply Psychology*, accessed January 27, 2025, https://www.simplypsychology.org
/maslow.html.

6 Michael L. Slepian and Drew S. Jacoby-Senghor, "Identity Threats in Everyday Life: Distinguishing Belonging from Inclusion," *Social Psychological and Personality Science* 12, no. 3 (2020): 392–406, https://
doi.org/10.1177/1948550619895008.

7 Leon Festinger, *A Theory of Cognitive Dissonance* (Stanford University Press, 1962).

8 Alison Wood Brooks and Leslie K. John, "The Surprising Power of Questions," *Harvard Business Review*, May–June 2018, https://hbr
.org/2018/05/the-surprising-power-of-questions.

9 Sheril Mathews, "Assertive Inquiry," *Leading Sapiens*, August 16, 2024, https://www.leadingsapiens.com/assertive-inquiry/.

10 Courtney Young-Law, "Leading through Ambiguity," *CORO Northern California*, June 22, 2020, https://coronorcal.org/2020/06/22
/leading-and-ambiguity/.

11 Peter M. Senge, *The Fifth Discipline: The Art and Practice of the Learning Organization* (Doubleday, 1990), 242–247.

Chapter 4

1 "Be Water, My Friend," *The Bruce Lee Podcast*, hosted by Shannon Lee, July 20, 2016, podcast audio, 49:16, https://brucelee.com /podcast-blog/2016/7/20/2-be-water-my-friend.

2 Toni Morrison, *Paradise* (Alfred A. Knopf, 1998), 125.

3 James M. Diefendorff and Gina A. Seaton, "Work Motivation," in *International Encyclopedia of the Social & Behavioral Sciences*, 2nd ed., (Elsevier, 2015), 680–686, https://doi.org/10.1016/B978-0-08 -097086-8.22036-9.

Chapter 5

1 Jeremy Sutton, "5 Benefits of Journaling for Mental Health," *Positive Psychology*, May 14, 2018, https://positivepsychology.com/benefits -of-journaling.

2 Rubina Veerakone, "Do We Only Use 10 Percent of Our Brain?" *McGovern Institute*, January 26, 2024, https://mcgovern.mit.edu /2024/01/26/do-we-use-only-10-percent-of-our-brain/.

3 James Baldwin, "As Much Truth as One Can Bear," *The New York Times Book Review*, January 14, 1962.

4 W. E. Hill, *My Wife and My Mother-in-Law*, 2015, in *Puck* 78, no. 2018: 11, image, https://www.loc.gov/pictures/item/2010652001/.

5 Beau Sievers et al. "Consensus-Building Conversation Leads to Neural Alignment," *Nature Communications* 15 (2024): 3936, https:// doi.org/10.1038/s41467-023-43253-8.

6 Edelman Trust Institute, *2024 Edelman Trust Barometer Global Report* (Edelman, 2024), https://www.edelman.com/trust/2024/trust-barometer.

7 Andrew Volmert and Nat Kendall-Taylor, "Most Americans Believe the 'System Is Rigged' against Them by Powerful Elites," *USA Today*, December 19, 2024, https://www.usatoday.com/story/opinion/2024 /12/19/united-healthcare-ceo-murder-frustration-health-insurance /77065837007/.

Chapter 7

1 Martin Luther King Jr., "Letter from Birmingham Jail," June 12, 1963, *Teaching American History*, accessed January 27, 2025, https:// teachingamericanhistory.org/document/letter-from-birmingham -city-jail-excerpts/.

2 Martin Luther King Jr., "The Birth of a New Age: Address Delivered on 11 August 1956 at the Fiftieth Anniversary of Alpha Phi Alpha in

Buffalo," *The Martin Luther King, Jr. Research and Education Institute*, accessed January 27, 2025, https://kinginstitute.stanford.edu /king-papers/documents/birth-new-age-address-delivered-11 -august-1956-fiftieth-anniversary-alpha-phi.

3 Raúl Alberto Mora, "Counter-Narrative," *Key Concepts in Intercultural Dialogue* 36, 2014, accessed January 27, 2025, https:// centerforinterculturaldialogue.org/wp-content/uploads/2014/10 /key-concept-counter-narrative.pdf.

4 A Seat at the Table, "Shirley Chisolm," *A Seat at the Table*, accessed January 27, 2025, https://www.bringyourownchair.org/about -shirley-chisholm/.

5 Shirley Chisholm, "Excerpts from the National Visionary Leadership Project," interview by Camille O. Cosby and Renee Poussaint, May 7, 2002, National Visionary Leadership Project, accessed January 27, 2025, https://awpc.cattcenter.iastate.edu/2017/03/09/excerpts -from-the-national-visionary-leadership-project-may-7-2002/.

6 Sam Dean, "Watch the Inventor of PR Explain How Bacon and Eggs Became an All-American Breakfast," *Bon Appétit*, June 8, 2012, https:// www.bonappetit.com/entertaining-style/pop-culture/article/watch -the-inventor-of-pr-explain-how-bacon-and-eggs-became-an-all -american-breakfast.

7 Katie Nodjimbadem, "The Trashy Beginnings of 'Don't Mess with Texas': A True Story of the Defining Phrase of the Lone Star State," *Smithsonian Magazine*, March 10, 2017, https://www.smithsonianmag .com/history/trashy-beginnings-dont-mess-texas-180962490/.

8 Frank Greve, "Curb Ramps Liberate Americans with Disabilities—and Everyone Else," *McClatchy Newspapers*, June 11, 2007, https://www .mcclatchydc.com/news/article24460762.html.

9 Angela Glover Blackwell, "The Curb-Cut Effect," *Stanford Social Innovation Review*, Winter 2017, https://ssir.org/articles/entry/the _curb_cut_effect.

10 The White House, "Fact Sheet: President Donald J. Trump Removes DEI from the Foreign Service," March 18, 2025, https://www.whitehouse .gov/fact-sheets/2025/03/fact-sheet-president-donald-j-trump -removes-dei-from-the-foreign-service/.

11 Narrative Arts, "What Is Public Narrative and How Can We Use It?" *Narrative Arts*, https://narrativearts.org/article/public -narrative/.

Chapter 8

1 Jay Kristoff, *Endsinger*, The Lotus War, Book 3 (New York: Thomas Dunne Books, 2014).

2 Elizabeth Linos, Sanaz Mobasseri, and Nina Roussille, *Intersectional Peer Effects at Work: The Effect of White Coworkers on Black Women's Careers*, Faculty Research Working Paper Series RWP23-031, Harvard Kennedy School, July 2024, accessed January 27, 2025, https://www.hks.harvard.edu/publications/intersectional-peer-effects-work-effect-white-coworkers-black-womens-careers.

Chapter 9

1 Anandi Mani et al., "Poverty Impedes Cognitive Function," *Science* 341, no. 6149 (2013): 976–980, https://doi.org/10.1126/science.1238041.

2 Amy Novotney, "The Psychology of Scarcity: Princeton Psychologist Eldar Shafir Explores How Deprivation Wreaks Havoc on Cognition and Decision-Making," *Monitor on Psychology* 45, no. 2 (2014): 28, https://www.apa.org/monitor/2014/02/scarcity.

3 Martin Luther King Jr., *Temple Israel of Hollywood Sermon*, speech, February 26, 1965, American Rhetoric, accessed January 27, 2025, https://www.americanrhetoric.com/speeches/mlktempleisrael hollywood.htm.

4 Smithsonian Institution, "Dr. Martin Luther King Jr.," accessed January 27, 2025, https://www.si.edu/spotlight/mlk.

5 Tom Murphy, "Most Americans Blame Insurance Profits and Coverage Denials alongside Killer in UnitedHealthcare CEO Death, Poll Finds," *PBS NewsHour*, December 27, 2024, https://www.pbs.org/newshour/politics/most-americans-blame-insurance-profits-and-coverage-denials-alongside-killer-in-unitedhealthcare-ceo-death-poll-finds.

6 Jay M. Feinman, *Delay, Deny, Defend: Why Insurance Companies Don't Pay Claims and What You Can Do about It* (Portfolio Hardcover, 2010).

7 Aimee Picchi, "Thousands of Los Angeles Homeowners Were Dropped by Their Insurers before the Palisades Fire," *CBS News*, January 20, 2025, https://www.cbsnews.com/news/fires-california-palisades-fire-homeowners-insurance-state-farm-fair-losses/.

8 Rachel Treisman, "Anthem Reverses Plans to Put Time Limits on Anesthesia Coverage," *NPR*, December 5, 2024, https://www.npr.org/2024/12/05/nx-s1-5217617/blue-cross-blue-shield-anesthesia-anthem.

9 Diane Belcher, "Leadership Fitness: Four Capacities Leaders Must Develop," *Harvard Business Publishing*, April 9, 2024, https://www.harvardbusiness.org/leadership-fitness-four-capacities-leaders-must-develop/.

10 Robert I. Sutton, "The Delicate Art of Being Perfectly Assertive," *Harvard Business Review*, June 28, 2010, https://hbr.org/2010/06/the-delicate-art-of-being-perf; Daniel R. Ames and Francis J. Flynn, "What Breaks a Leader: The Curvilinear Relation between Assertiveness and Leadership," *Journal of Personality and Social Psychology* 92, no. 2 (2007): 307–324, https://www.columbia.edu/~da358/publications/ames_flynn_assertiveness.pdf.

Chapter 10

1 IDEO U, "The Beginner's Guide to Systems Thinking: Core Mindsets for Seeing the Big Picture," *IDEO U*, accessed January 27, 2025, https://www.ideou.com/blogs/inspiration/beginners-guide-systems-thinking-core-mindsets; Arne Collen and Gianfranco Minati, "Seven Activities to Engage Systems Thinking," 1999, https://www.arnecollen.com/wp-content/uploads/2012/07/Seven-Activities_AC_GM_99.pdf.

2 Simon Sinek, *The Infinite Game* (Portfolio, 2019); Bernard De Koven, *The Well-Played Game: A Player's Philosophy* (MIT Press, 2013).

Conclusion

1 Eduardo Bonilla-Silva, *Racism without Racists: Color-Blind Racism and the Persistence of Racial Inequality in America*, 6th ed. (Rowman & Littlefield, 2021).

FURTHER READING

I was and am continually intrigued and/or inspired by the following books, which I wholeheartedly recommend:

The Authoritarian Personality by Theodor W. Adorno, Else Frenkel-Brunswik, Daniel Levinson, and R. Nevitt Sanford (Harper & Row, 1950)

White Rage: The Unspoken Truth of Our Racial Divide by Carol Anderson (Bloomsbury, 2016)

Propaganda by Edward Bernays (Horace Liveright, 1928)

The Way Out: How to Overcome Toxic Polarization by Peter T. Coleman (Columbia University Press, 2021)

A Theory of Cognitive Dissonance by Leon Festinger (Stanford University Press, 1957)

Leadership on the Line: Staying Alive Through the Dangers of Change by Ronald A. Heifetz and Marty Linsky (Harvard Business Review Press, 2017)

Manufacturing Consent: The Political Economy of the Mass Media by Edward S. Herman and Noam Chomsky (Pantheon Books, 1988)

The Managed Heart: Commercialization of Human Feeling, 3rd ed., by Arlie Russell Hochschild (University of California Press, 2012)

We Do This 'Til We Free Us: Abolitionist Organizing and Transforming Justice by Mariame Kaba (Haymarket Books, 2021)

Thinking, Fast and Slow by Daniel Kahneman (Farrar, Straus and Giroux, 2011)

The Wake Up: Closing the Gap Between Good Intentions and Real Change by Michelle MiJung Kim (Balance, 2021)

The Master's Tools Will Never Dismantle the Master's House by Audre Lorde (Penguin Books, 2018)

Toward a Psychology of Being, 3rd ed., by Abraham Maslow (Wiley, 1998)

On Tyranny: Twenty Lessons from the Twentieth Century by Timothy Snyder (Tim Duggan Books, 2017)

The Protestant Ethic and the Spirit of Capitalism by Max Weber, trans. Stephen Kalberg (Penguin Classics, 2002)

DAILY REFLECTION CHECKLIST

Questions to Guide Your Growth

This checklist outlines key dimensions, promising practices, and daily reflective questions that inspire meaningful change.

PART I: THINK

> **Goal:** Question what you believe and learn about history and social influences to solve problems durably.
>
> **Ask yourself:** What assumptions am I making today, and how can I challenge them to see a broader perspective?
>
> ☐ **Promising Practice 1:** *Change Your Mind before You Change the System*
> Examine how your thinking has been shaped by social cues and unconscious bias, so you can intentionally disrupt default beliefs and make space for liberatory perspectives.
>
> **Ask yourself:** What belief or assumption did I act on today without questioning—and what might shift if I saw it differently? Where did that belief come from?
>
> ☐ **Promising Practice 2:** *Bite the Frog, Beat the Avoidance*
> Confront discomfort rather than avoid it, recognizing that avoidance—especially of hard truths—upholds the status quo and delays meaningful change.

Ask yourself: What uncomfortable truth or difficult conversation am I avoiding today—and what might shift if I faced it head-on?

☐ **Promising Practice 3: *Ask Questions That Slay***
Use inquiry as a tool for equity—ask bold, thoughtful, and inclusive questions that challenge assumptions, deepen understanding, and drive more just outcomes through a balance of advocacy and curiosity.

Ask yourself: What question did I ask—or avoid asking—today that could have opened the door to a deeper truth or a more inclusive perspective? Have I asked at least one more question to gain new insights?

☐ **Promising Practice 4: *Don't Let Assumptions Run the Show***
Use the Ladder of Inference to slow down and examine how unconscious biases and assumptions shape your decisions, so you can choose responses rooted in clarity, equity, and curiosity rather than default judgment.

Ask yourself: What assumptions did I make today, and how might they have limited my perspective or actions?

PART II: FEEL

Goal: Pay attention to how you feel. Understand your emotions and use them to connect with others and make positive changes.

Ask yourself: How am I truly feeling right now, and how can I use this awareness to connect more authentically with others?

☐ **Promising Practice 5:** *How's Your Spirit?*
Pause and check in with your emotional and mental state, asking yourself if you feel aligned with your values, capable, and meaningfully connected, so you can lead with courage, not just compliance.

Ask yourself: What emotions am I experiencing, and what are they telling me about my needs? What do I need to feel more aligned, brave, and grounded in who I am?

☐ **Promising Practice 6:** *No Crying over Spilled Milk*
Consistently journal to uncover patterns, challenge long-held beliefs (a.k.a. "sacred cows"), and create space for fresh perspectives, proving that even the tools we resist can lead to powerful transformation.

Ask yourself: How can I capture a creative thought or moment from today to inspire future ideas? What did I notice today that I hadn't seen before, and what belief or behavior might I need to rethink because of it?

☐ **Promising Practice 7:** *Reframe It Like You Mean It*
Use asset-based framing to shift from skepticism to possibility, transforming discomfort, bias, or difference into opportunities for connection, learning, and collective progress.

Ask yourself: What strengths or opportunities can I highlight to make the most of today? Where did I feel resistance today, and how might reframing it reveal a new possibility or point of connection?

PART III: DO

Goal: Take steps to make a difference. Practice being a good leader, standing up for yourself, and thinking about how things are connected.

Ask yourself: What one intentional action can I take today to align my behaviors with my values and goals?

☐ **Promising Practice 8:** *Clap Back with Narrative*
Use counter-narratives to challenge dominant power structures, center marginalized voices, and reclaim storytelling as a tool for truth, accountability, and justice.

Ask yourself: What dominant narrative did I encounter today, and how could a counter-narrative reveal a deeper truth or shift the conversation toward equity? What dominant story can I challenge today by amplifying a different perspective?

☐ **Promising Practice 9:** *Curiosity on Purpose*
Turn curiosity into a deliberate strategy for equity, using deep questioning, disruption, and learning from setbacks to challenge assumptions, spark innovation, and drive meaningful, lasting change.

Ask yourself: What assumption can I examine today, and how might staying curious help me uncover something I might have missed?

☐ **Promising Practice 10:** *A Fitness Exam*
Assess and strengthen four essential capacities—balance, strength, flexibility, and endurance—needed to lead with clarity, courage, and impact in complex, equity-focused environments.

Ask yourself: Which leadership muscle did I stretch today, and which one needs more attention to help me lead with purpose and integrity?

☐ **Promising Practice 11: *Be Perfectly Assertive***
Emphasize clear, respectful communication that balances empathy with accountability, empowering leaders to address harm, set expectations, and lead with both compassion and conviction.

Ask yourself: Did I speak up with both clarity and care today? How did my communication reinforce accountability and respect?

PART IV: REVISIT

Goal: Determine what you want to start/stop/continue. Keep improving and finding new ways to grow.

Ask yourself: What did I learn today that I can use to improve tomorrow?

☐ **Promising Practice 12: *Don't Hate the Player, Hate the Game***
Use systems thinking to recognize how rules, roles, and communication shape outcomes so you can challenge inequitable dynamics, redesign systems for inclusion, and shift from passive participation to purposeful transformation.

Ask yourself: Subtraction can be additive, so what can I subtract today that would add value to at least one system? What rule, pattern, or assumption within it deserves to be challenged or rewritten?

ACKNOWLEDGMENTS

To my husband, Jonathan, and daughter, Audrey: You are my safe place, my loudest cheerleaders, my first readers, and my fiercest supporters. Audrey, in that perfectly serious, wise-beyond-your-years five-year-old voice, you once said, "The strongest shape in the world is a triangle, and we are a triangle family—so we are the strongest." You were right, kid. I love you both, 3,000. You love me more, but I love you most. Infinity. Googleplex. I win!

To my seven siblings, and to mom and dad (rest in power): Thank you for the early adventures—the chaos, the love, the lessons—that shaped so much of who I am and who I continue to become. As the eldest daughter and unofficial family manager, I'm grateful for the laughter, the disagreements, and all the relentless teasing along the way. And yes, I'm still the boss . . . no matter what any of you say.

To my editor and friend, Jeevan Sivasubramaniam, thank you for seeing the spark in a budding idea and stoking it into a fire. This book might have happened without you *eventually*, but it wouldn't have hit the same. I'll never forget the day you pulled my proposal from the slush pile and—*unheard of*—called me immediately. You said, "This is the kind of book I got into publishing for." Your belief in this project and your unshakeable enthusiasm lit a fire under me, and for that, I am forever grateful.

To the entire Berrett-Koehler team, I chose you because of your unwavering commitment to justice, to "good trouble," and to curating authors who want to shake the world up and build it back better. You're the Beyoncé of publishing teams, and I wouldn't want to work with anyone else. Thank you for turning my lifelong dream into a reality and for making it *fun* along the way.

To Shari and Darce Slate: Writing while listening to the crashing waves? Perfection. Thank you for opening your home and your hearts to me. One day, I'll find a way to repay your kindness, but until then, I promise to pay it forward.

To my Sonoma County Writers' Camp friends: Y'all are my writing soulmates. Thank you for listening to my stories and sharing yours. The lessons I've learned from you—and the community we've built—mean the world to me. I'll see you at the next retreat, barefoot, with notebooks in hand and wine glasses ready.

To my community of family and friends (too many to name; you know who you are): Thank you for every hug, every late-night phone call, every meme and reel that had me laughing when I needed it most. Thank you for the check-in texts, the shared tears, and the grace you gave me when I went radio silent to get this book written. As to the writing of this book, a few honorable mentions cannot go without being named for all they poured into me and this project—thanks to Ashley Atkins, Jess Dekker, Sharon Cho, La Vida Johnson, David Newcomb, Sophia Sindalovsky, Helene Sims, Ambreia Meadows-Fernandez, Jennifer Barrett, Bonni Stachowiak, Naima McQueen, Kia Fay, Dr. Janice Gassam Asare, Samya France, Suzzette Martinez-Malavet, Misha Gutierrez, Abbie Griffith, Dr. Nana Afoh-Manin, Shane Dolgin, and Shruti Kothari. I'm so ready to get back to our friend dates, hikes, and community activism. And you already know—my favorite thing to do is hood rat shit with my friends.

To my mentors and sponsors along the way: Thank you for every lesson, every piece of advice, and every open door. Your belief in me has been a foundation for everything I've built, and I carry your lessons with me in all that I do.

This book is for all of you—and for everyone who dares to step into the world boldly, unapologetically, and ready to change it.

INDEX

ABOUT THE AUTHOR

AMIRA BARGER is an award-winning executive vice president at one of the world's largest communications and public relations firms. She leads DEI Advisory and provides communications counsel globally. With over twenty years of experience in strategic communications, Amira is a recognized scholar-practitioner and thought leader who blends innovation and impact to inspire change.

She has been featured in the Associated Press, Reuters, *Business Insider*, *EdSource*, *Essence*, *Forbes*, *HR Executive*, *Parents*, ABC Bay Area, CBS Bay Area, CNBC, KQED, and NBC Bay Area, among others. A regular contributor to MSNBC and *Fast Company*, Amira shares insights on leadership, organizational health, behavioral communications, and DEI, with a passion for driving transformation.

Amira has earned numerous accolades, including being named Woman of the Year by Women Health Care Executives and a Fearlessly Authentic Leader by Leaderology as well as one of the Top 50 Women to Watch for Corporate Boards by 50/50 Women on Boards, Top 100 Executives by INvolve People, Top CMOs of 2024 by the CMO Alliance, Top 50 Global DEI

Professionals by OnConferences, Top 100 People Leaders by Mogul, and 30 Under 40 in Healthcare Innovation by *Business Insider*.

She is a dedicated educator who serves as a professor of marketing, communications, and change management at California State University, East Bay and as a lecturer at the University of California, San Francisco. In her teaching, she draws on her data-driven approach and design-thinking expertise to prepare future leaders to navigate complex challenges and foster equity in their organizations and the community.

Amira holds a BA in marketing from Vanguard University, an MBA from LeTourneau University, and multiple DEI certifications from Cornell University, the University of South Florida, and SDS Global Enterprises Inc. She is a Certified Volunteer Administrator (CVA) and Certified Fund Raising Executive (CFRE), reflecting her commitment to lifelong learning and growth.

Deeply invested in her community, Amira serves on multiple nonprofit boards. In their spare time, her family explores US national parks and monuments, with plans to visit all 417.

Amira lives in Benicia, CA, with her life partner of over twenty years, Jonathan, their daughter Audrey, and their two dogs, Bucky, a silver Labrador, and Potato, a toy poodle-ish rescue mutt.

amirabarger.com

Berrett–Koehler
Publishers

Berrett-Koehler is an independent publisher dedicated to an ambitious mission: *Connecting people and ideas to create a world that works for all.*

Our publications span many formats, including print, digital, audio, and video. We also offer online resources, training, and gatherings. And we will continue expanding our products and services to advance our mission.

We believe that the solutions to the world's problems will come from all of us, working at all levels: in our society, in our organizations, and in our own lives. Our publications and resources offer pathways to creating a more just, equitable, and sustainable society. They help people make their organizations more humane, democratic, diverse, and effective (and we don't think there's any contradiction there). And they guide people in creating positive change in their own lives and aligning their personal practices with their aspirations for a better world.

And we strive to practice what we preach through what we call "The BK Way." At the core of this approach is *stewardship,* a deep sense of responsibility to administer the company for the benefit of all of our stakeholder groups, including authors, customers, employees, investors, service providers, sales partners, and the communities and environment around us. Everything we do is built around stewardship and our other core values of *quality, partnership, inclusion,* and *sustainability.*

We are grateful to our readers, authors, and other friends who are supporting our mission. We ask you to share with us examples of how BK publications and resources are making a difference in your lives, organizations, and communities at bkconnection.com/impact.

Dear reader,

Thank you for picking up this book and welcome to the worldwide BK community! You're joining a special group of people who have come together to create positive change in their lives, organizations, and communities.

What's BK all about?

Our mission is to connect people and ideas to create a world that works for all.

Why? Our communities, organizations, and lives get bogged down by old paradigms of self-interest, exclusion, hierarchy, and privilege. But we believe that can change. That's why we seek the leading experts on these challenges—and share their actionable ideas with you.

A welcome gift

To help you get started, we'd like to offer you a **free copy** of one of our bestselling ebooks:

bkconnection.com/welcome

When you claim your **free ebook**, you'll also be subscribed to our blog.

Our freshest insights

Access the best new tools and ideas for leaders at all levels on our blog at ideas.bkconnection.com.

Sincerely,

Your friends at Berrett-Koehler